PRAYERS FOR PILGRIMS

Margaret Pawley was born in Germany of
British parents, and has lived in many countries
in the course of her life, including wartime
service with the SOE in Egypt and Italy. She read
History at Oxford and has been much involved
in adult education in Britain and abroad; for
some years a tutor at the Open University.
Having lived in a number of Cathedral settings,
including Ely and St Paul's, her home is now in
Canterbury. She is a member of the British
Regional Committee for St George's College,
Jerusalem. Her books include a study of
Anglican-Roman Catholic relations, a bio-
graphy of Donald Coggan and a collection of
prayers, *Praying With the English Tradition*,
while she has also edited two volumes of
sermons by Robert Runcie.

PRAYERS FOR PILGRIMS

Compiled and introduced by
Margaret Pawley

Foreword by David Adam

First published 1991
Triangle
SPCK
Holy Trinity Church
Marylebone Road
London NW1 4DU

British Library Cataloguing in Publication Data

Prayers for pilgrims.
1. Christian life. Prayer
I. Pawley, Margaret
248.32

ISBN 0-281-04507-0

Typeset by Rowland Phototypesetting Ltd
Bury St Edmunds, Suffolk
Printed in Great Britain by
BPCC Hazell Books
Aylesbury, Bucks
Member of BPCC Ltd

Contents

Foreword

We are all on the move; we are all travelling through time and through space. No one can stand still for long, or stay in exactly the same area. We are all caught up in what someone has called the 'dance of Creation'. From great galaxies to atoms, all are in constant motion. Part of existence is to be in motion, and to be truly alive is to be aware of that motion. What we have to decide at some time or other is: where are we going? Has our journey a purpose or a goal? Are we journeying somewhere as pilgrims or are we just drifting in space?

At the end of a century in which we find it so easy to dispense with the wisdom of the past, it is not surprising that for over twenty years we have been singing:

> I'm a real nowhere man,
> making all my nowhere plans . . .

For many today, life has no direction, no purpose or meaning. So many people today seem to be constantly rushing from one place to another. They consume mile after mile, they burn petrol, they eat up scenery, but are hardly satisfied and do not know when they have arrived; they move on relentlessly, fulfilling some inner call.

To such people I want to say, go on pilgrimage – make purposeful journeys. Learn that you are not alone; many others have made such journeys before you, and they have left some guidance for you to follow. Seek out places that are special because of heroic deeds of faith, or that have been sanctified by holy lives. Discover those who died *for* something, rather than *of* something, people who journeyed with a purpose. Seek out the places that will become special for you, places where the distant becomes close and where the reality of the divine presence becomes a little more apparent. Places where the divide between heaven and earth has grown thin through the prayers of the faithful. There rest awhile, and seek to let your vision be restored.

There is a theme of travelling to a purpose which runs throughout the whole Bible. Abraham heeded the call to leave his native land, to abandon the safe and familiar for the adventure of the great Unknown; he did not know where he was going but he knew, or at least was searching for, the God who was going with him. Moses, when he was wavering, was reminded by God that in all the journey, 'My presence shall go with you and I will give you rest.' To which Moses replied, 'If your presence does not go with me, carry me not hence' (Exodus 33.14–15). Here is a recognition that pilgrimage is a journey with God and into God. A reminder that we do not travel the road alone, but that he walks with us in the way.

By the very nature of our creation God calls us forward. When we heed the call of God, we know we are on pilgrimage. In a poem entitled 'Pilgrimage', G. R. D. McLean wrote:

> . . . God our pilgrimage impels
> To cross sea-waste or scale life-fells;
> A further shore,
> One hill-brow more,
> Draws on the feet, or arm-plied oars,
> As the soul onward, upward soars.

Beyond the hills a wider plain,
Beyond the waves the Isle domain
   With richness blest
   A place for guest,
Where God doth sit upon his throne,
The soul by Christ nor left alone.

St Columbanus said, 'Home is not a place but a road to be travelled.' This did not make him homeless, for wherever he went he found his Father's house. With such an attitude the whole universe takes on a new meaning. Though we may be uncertain of the place we are going to, or of what lies ahead, we know that he will be there to meet us. If we do not know him, all the greater need for us to heed the call to become, in the lovely ancient phrase, 'pilgrims for the love of God'. If our faith is weak, we need all the more to seek to travel in depth and make the journey inwards.

But although God is present always and everywhere, we still need to go to a special place where, once we have discovered God there, we discover he is everywhere. Sometimes we need to return to that special place so that we may strengthen our vision which is becoming dim, and reaffirm our faith that is weakening. Notice how God asked Jacob to return to Bethel (Genesis 35.1), the place of his vision, so that there his vision might be renewed. Jacob returned in order that in the 'House of God' he might get strength for the tasks ahead. There is a need for us all to have a 'House of God' or a 'Holy Island', a place of pilgrimage, where we can go to be refreshed and renewed. It is important that we do discover for ourselves such 'holy ground', so that all of life may be consecrated by it.

So I recommend that you find and go to a holy

place. But if you are unable to do so, you can still travel inward. For example, the Stations of the Cross are visited regularly by thousands who have never walked the Via Dolorosa or seen the streets of Jerusalem. They travel in their imagination and in their spirit. They use images, words, art and sculpture to help them visit each place that Jesus travelled on the way to the Cross. There is no distance that prevents such a journey, only our unwillingness to travel it in depth. This book is a call to come on pilgrimage for the love of God, to heed his call, to travel with God and into God. Discover what it is like to be a pilgrim; come and travel the road with those who have gone before.

Make this book a useful travelling companion to the holy places, but if Rome is too far away, or you are prevented from crossing the causeway to Holy Island, then still let it help you on the inner journey. Follow the pilgrim route from Iona to Lindisfarne, from Lindisfarne to Durham, and on to York. Alternatively, journey to Taizé, on to Assisi and to Rome. You can visit St David's in south-west Wales and capture a feel of the Celtic outpost, or travel to Canterbury, hallowed by pilgrims down the centuries. Visit Julian's shrine at Norwich, or the shrine of our Lady at Walsingham. Cross the seas with the pilgrims to America. Take up the 'scallop shell of quiet' and the 'staff of faith to walk upon'. Wherever you are, take time to be a pilgrim. Travel with a purpose. Get the feel for places through the prayers of this book, and by learning of the lives of the holy men and women who have gone before you. Seek to discover the excitement of such a journey, for those who make it will never be the same again. Such a journey will take an effort, but it will reward all who are willing to 'thrust out a little from the land'. Seek to capture the joy of the journey, a joy such as Emily Dickinson expresses in setting out to sea.

> Exultation is the going
> Of an inland soul to sea –
> Past the houses,
> Past the headlands,
> Into deep Eternity.

God bless you with His Presence, that in your journey you may find joy, and in your pilgrimage peace.

DAVID ADAM
Lindisfarne

Introduction

The idea of pilgrimage is much older than Christianity, but always it has been an expression of the same two main concepts: that of *making* a pilgrimage by travelling to a specific geographical site, and that of *being* on a perpetual pilgrimage; the journey is life itself. Both are the pursuit of a greater good than mere existence, and both involve discomfort and hardship, if not a much overworked word, peril. To view life as a pilgrimage is, in part, a description of life as the result of living it. (Here belong Mrs Willis's 'steep and rugged pathway' (p. 46) and the 'mazes of this world' of Erasmus (p. 26)).

But only in part, for through all ages an innate sense of longing has shown itself in the hearts of men and women for a better world beyond the present: where the meaning of existence, of the seemingly arbitrary nature of many current happenings, will become clear; where there is justice, peace, love. For Christians, that is the realm where God is shown forth as Creator and Father of all, the origin of his revelation of himself, in time, in the sonship of Jesus Christ – the same Jesus who said to his disciples, 'I go to prepare a place for you.' In our present limited comprehension, we call this habitation heaven, the heavenly Jerusalem.

The longing for heaven has been vividly described, in the Letter to the Hebrews, as the experience of certain prophets and patriarchs:

> . . . All these persons died in faith. They were not yet in possession of the things promised, but had

seen them far ahead and hailed them, and confessed themselves no more than strangers or passing travellers on earth. Those who use such language show plainly that they are looking for a country of their own . . . we find them longing for a better country – I mean the heavenly one. (Hebrews 11.13–16 NEB)

The metaphor of heaven as a country or a city to be reached occurs much in pilgrimage prayers, following the earlier reference in Hebrews to Abraham 'looking forward to the city with firm foundations whose architect and builder is God' (11.10).

Two examples occur in well-known hymns:

> Land me safe on Canaan's side.

and

> Marching to the promised land.

The English language lacks an adequate term for this state of mind; German has the word *sehnsucht* – yearning-search. St Augustine comes close: 'Our hearts are restless till they find their rest in thee.'

Modern poets recognise this exilic quality in mankind's nature. Geoffrey Hill writes:

> Exile or pilgrim set me once more upon that ground;
> my rich and desolate childhood . . .[1]

Though often beautifully phrased, the holy discontent with the earthly *status quo* expressed in many prayers for life as pilgrimage, has frequently given voice to a spirit of melancholy. Recent moves to associate so-called 'Kingdom theology' with pilgrimage, and with Christians as a pilgrim people, have come to the rescue.

Jesus did not explain what the Kingdom of God

was; he brought it in himself. It was an experience and a community associated with him. Although the Kingdom of God is completed in resurrection, it is a present possession as well as a future inheritance. Within these terms we find that the final destination of the earthly pilgrimage lessens in importance in relation to that of the *journey*: not the cold implementation of concepts, but walking in company with the Lord; looking for the will of the King who shares the daily struggle, decisions and suffering along the way in our search for love and justice, the signs of the Kingdom won by the cross; what Professor Jürgen Moltmann has called 'Kingdom of God work'. Boethius sums up this more positive and less dualistic view of pilgrimage with his equal emphasis: 'Thou art the journey and the journey's end' (p. 19). Further prayers which reflect a similar spirit find their place in this collection.

Pilgrimages to specific places began in earliest times. The motives of pilgrims have been mixed: the expiation of guilt, the expectation of miracle or, under older systems of moral theology, the acquisition of merit. At lowest, pilgrimages provided the opportunity to travel and to satisfy curiosity, especially at times when movement was regulated by law (under the feudal system people were much confined to their own localities); at highest they represented the quest for holiness. In many pilgrim sites men and women have come to recognise the Fatherhood of God and have stayed to worship. As the result of faith revealed and prayer offered, these places have acquired an atmosphere altogether unique. T. S. Eliot found it so at Little Gidding (p. 79); for others, St David's Cathedral, the Abbey Church on Iona and the ruins of St Cuthbert's monastery on Lindisfarne, in particular, speak to the soul and heart. Pilgrimages in this spirit flourish today to a wide variety of sites throughout the world. Prayers in this book are offered as a starting point.

The *shared* nature of the pilgrim experience has no doubt a powerful influence. On pilgrimage, that worst of human sorrows, loneliness, is removed; interdependence and mutual love are emphasised. Langland recognised this in his *The Vision of Piers Plowman*, written about 1362:

> We should be humble and kind and faithful to
>   each other,
> And long-suffering like pilgrims, for pilgrims are
>   we all.

'Brother clasps the hand of brother' as a sign of support and encouragement, in the well-known hymn 'Through the night of doubt and sorrow on-ward goes the pilgrim band'. (Sisters, unaided it would appear, need to step even more fearlessly!)

Opposition to pilgrimages to the Holy Land came early from at least two specific sources: the first was from Eusebius, Bishop of Caesarea from *c.* 315.[2] He resisted making a holy place the focus of devotion, maintaining that it would suggest that God's work was limited to Palestine, in a small corner of the world only. Once Jesus was risen, his work was universal, and this fact would be blurred by concentration on one area; believers would be encouraged to look backwards into history, rather than forward to the 'glorious expectation of the Jerusalem that is above'. Gregory, Bishop of Nyssa in Cappadocia from about 371, was equally trenchant when he wrote, 'When the Lord invites the blessed to their inheritance in the kingdom of heaven, he does not include a pilgrimage to Jerusalem amongst the good things they are to do.' I have tried to heed these warnings in making my selection of prayers for pilgrimage to the Holy Land and to take a forward, as well as a historical view. To pose the other side of the argument, there can be few pilgrims who have not experienced the coming alive of the Scriptures, as they travel to the lakeside, the lanes, hills and villages of the land known to Jesus.

Reaction to pilgrimage in England in the sixteenth century was sharp and to be expected, for Reformation theology was suspicious of superstition and idolatry and both could be detected in the custom of pilgrimage. By the beginning of the nineteenth century, archeologists had begun seriously to excavate ancient sites in Egypt and Palestine. Attitudes were often uncomprehending and insular towards the cultures they uncovered; in particular towards fellow-Christians of other traditions such as Greeks, Russians, Armenians and Copts, still worshipping in the land of the common heritage. A poem of 1841, entitled *The Pilgrimage*, illustrates this view:

I bow not, therefore, in the gorgeous pile
Where golden lamps irradiate the gloom,
And monks their votaries and themselves beguile
To think they worship at their Saviour's tomb.
. . .
This be the reverence paid, the homage shown —
Well had its site remained unnoticed and
    unknown.[3]

Happily, a new climate of greater tolerance and appreciation of different Christian customs has come about. My choice of pilgrimage prayers for the Holy Land reflects this welcome change; moreover, pilgrimages on an inter-Church basis can do much further to remove prejudice. But the reaction to the past was not all loss, for from it came a fresh concept of the possibility of *interior* pilgrimage. An example, from an unexpected source, came from a schoolboy's prize poem, read to Rugby School on 29 March 1837.

> The pilgrims sleep; their toil, their pain, is now
> A tale and nothing more; on Zion's hill
> The staff, the sackcloth, and the saddened brow
> Are seen no longer; and the vow is still,
> And silence dwells in Salem's citadel;
> Yet still on earth, a pilgrim band, like them
> With Faith our staff and Love our scallop shell,
> Through life and death our weary way we stem
> Up to our holier hill, our true Jerusalem.[4]

The prayers in this book follow the various patterns of pilgrimage that have been mentioned; though placed in categories and under headings, many are interchangeable. In the 1990s the journey comes in many guises: we may regard the whole of life as a pilgrimage, and so live it out; we may see ourselves as walking with Jesus, trying to help to establish his Kingdom; we may travel as pilgrims to Galilee, to Bec, to Taizé, Walsingham, Ely or Glastonbury, to taste their riches; or we need go no further than our own armchair, there to pray in our common vocation as pilgrims, guided by memory or holy imagination.

It has been my intention to make the sources of these prayers are broad as possible: the fruits of the experience of Roman Catholics, Orthodox, Free Church men and women, as well as Anglicans. I have also tried to cover a wide time-span. There have been some surprises in discovering the rich imagery that has been used to describe pilgrimage; particularly the frequency of a common figurative use of *water*. It is to be expected from the Hebrides, but unexpected from Ann Griffiths, deep into Wales, who may never have seen the sea. Even St Basil and St Augustine use watery metaphors, as do prayers from Africa and Asia. Other pilgrims tread dry land: 'Let me see your footmarks and in them plant mine own', for example. Edward Taylor's pilgrims (p. 103) are privileged and travel with wheels:

> For in Christ's coach they sweetly sing,
> As they to glory ride within.

Some of the prayers are deliberately intended to be familiar; others new.

Prayers for pilgrims to the Holy Land were gathered for the most part during a three-week visit to Jerusalem in the spring of 1990, although the search for the fifteenth-century Processionals, written by the Franciscans of Mount Sion, mentioned in so many mediaeval pilgrimage accounts, proved fruitless. Great, therefore, was my excitement, when the Bodleian Library in Oxford was found to possess *Un guide du pèlerin de Terre Sainte au XVe siècle*, a book in French, published in 1940. Its author had found an ancient and tiny leather-bound volume, only a few inches long, containing the Processionals, in a collector's library up for sale, and had proceeded to transcribe the Latin pilgrimage prayers. I have included several of them, translated into English. There were other happy experiences: the search for prayers of those who travelled to the New World as pilgrims in the seventeenth century brought me in touch with a rich tradition of which, in my ignorance, I had previously been unaware.

I had a mind to include a pilgrim's prayer from Russia, for pilgrimage has long been part of that tradition. The 'Jesus prayer' is used almost exclusively. Metropolitan Anthony of Sourozh has said of this prayer: 'The doctrinal and spiritual wealth of the

Jesus prayer is infinite; it is both a summary and the whole of the faith whose enigma is solved in Christ.'[5] Central to the prayer in the name of Jesus is man's aim – 'his vocation of union with God'.[6]

As this seems to say it all, I end with the prayer:

> O Lord Jesus Christ, Son of God,
> have mercy upon me:

and with an extract from a letter of St Jerome:[7]

> By the Cross I mean not the wood but the Passion. That Cross is in Britain, in India, in the whole world. Happy is he who carries in his own heart the Cross, the Resurrection, the place of the Nativity and of the Ascension.

MARGARET PAWLEY
Canterbury

1 Geoffrey Hill, 'The Coming of Offa', from *Collected Poems* (Penguin 1959).
2 See Peter Walker, *Holy City, Holy Places* (OUP 1990).
3 F. S. Egerton (1800–57), poet and statesman, first Earl of Ellesmere, 1846.
4 R. Congreve.
5 In his Introduction to *The Way of a Pilgrim*, trs. R. M. French (Triangle 1986).
6 ibid.
7 *c.* 342–420; he lived for many years in Bethlehem, translating the Bible into Latin. This extract comes from Epistle 58.

THE PILGRIMAGE
OF LIFE

The Pilgrim

Give me my scallop-shell of quiet,
My staff of faith to walk upon,
My scrip of joy, immortal diet,
My bottle of salvation,
My gown of glory, hope's true gage;
And thus I'll take my pilgrimage . . .

And this is my eternal plea,
To him that made Heaven, Earth and Sea,
Seeing my flesh must die so soon . . .
Then am I ready like a palmer fit,
To tread those blest paths which before I writ.

SIR WALTER RALEIGH c. *1552–1618, explorer and colonizer. He wrote a good deal of poetry, much of which has been lost; this poem is considered to have been written during imprisonment before his execution.

No fear in unknown ways

O Holy Spirit,
    whose presence is liberty,
grant us that freedom of the Spirit
    which will not fear to tread in unknown ways,
nor be held back by misgivings of ourselves
    and fear of others.
Ever beckon us forward to the place of your will,
    which is also the place of your power,
O ever-leading, ever-loving Lord.

GEORGE APPLETON, *b. 1902, a distinguished modern writer and compiler of prayers, was Archbishop of Perth from 1963 to 1969 and Archbishop in Jerusalem from 1969 to 1974.*

Be thou the goal of my pilgrimage

O thou full of compassion,
I commit and commend myself unto thee,
    in whom I am,
    and live,
    and know.
Be thou the goal of my pilgrimage,
    and my rest by the way.
Let my soul take refuge
    from the crowding turmoil
    of worldly thoughts
    beneath the shadow of thy wings;
let my heart, this sea of restless waves,
    find peace in thee, O God.
Thou bounteous giver of all good gifts,
    give to him who is weary refreshing food;
gather our distracted thoughts and powers
    into harmony again;
    and set the prisoner free.
See, he stands at thy door and knocks;
    be it opened to him,
    that he may enter with a free step,
    and be quickened by thee.
For thou art the well-spring of life,
    the light of eternal brightness,
    wherein the just live
    who love thee.
Be it unto me according to thy word.

ST AUGUSTINE 354–430 was born in North Africa and studied
at the university of Carthage. He left for Rome, still a pagan, and
went on to Milan where he came under the influence of the bishop,
Ambrose. He was baptised on Easter Eve 387. Returning to North
Africa, became first assistant bishop, and then Bishop of Hippo.

A country far beyond the stars

My soul, there is a country
   Far beyond the stars,
Where stands a wingèd sentry
   All skilful in the wars.

There, above noise and danger,
   Sweet peace sits, crowned with smiles,
And one born in a manger
   Commands the beauteous files.

He is thy gracious friend,
   And – O my soul, awake! –
Did in pure love descend,
   To die here for thy sake.

If thou canst get but thither,
   There grows the flower of peace,
The rose that cannot wither,
   Thy fortress and thy ease.

Leave then thy foolish ranges,
   For none can thee secure
But one, who never changes,
   Thy God, thy life, thy cure.

HENRY VAUGHAN 1622–95, poet and doctor from the country-side of Brecon. He wrote much religious poetry which included a collection called 'Silex Scintillans' from which this extract is taken.

Lead me, that I may do your work

O God our Father
And his son Jesu Christ
And the Holy Spirit,
May you give me a blessing while in this world,
while you lead me through the forests,
through the lakes and the mountains,
So that I may do your work among your people.
Grant that I may be loved by you,
and your people.

*This prayer was written in the Luganda language at the back of
the diary of a martyr and found after his death.*

Let your spirit be my sail

O Jesus,
Be the canoe that holds me to the sea of life.
Be the steer that keeps me on the straight road.
Be the outrigger that supports me in times of great
     temptation.
Let your spirit be my sail that carries me through
     every day.
Keep my body strong,
so that I can paddle steadfastly on,
   in the long voyage of life.

A prayer from the New Hebrides, exact source unknown.

No port of anchorage in this world

O God,
   whose eternal providence
   has embarked our souls in the ship of our bodies,
not to expect any port of anchorage
   on the sea of this world,
   but to steer through it
   to thy glorious kingdom,
Preserve us, O Lord,
   from the dangers that on all sides assault us,
and keep our affections still fitly disposed
   to receive thy holy inspirations;
that, being carried sweetly and strongly forward
   by thy Holy Spirit,
we may arrive at last
   in the haven where we would be;
through Jesus Christ our Lord.

GEORGE HICKES 1642–1715. *A man of piety and scholarship, having taken on oath of allegiance to James II, he refused to take a similar oath to William and Mary; he was deprived of his deanery at Worcester, but was later consecrated titular Bishop of Thetford by the Non-jurors.*

Help us to walk

O Lord,
Through you our children will have strong hearts,
    and they will walk the straight path
        in a sacred manner.
Help me to walk the sacred path of life
        without difficulty,
    with my mind and heart continually
        fixed on you.

To learn new ways

O God, we pray to you amid the perplexities
        of a changing order.
Help us to learn new ways that you would teach us,
    and in every unknown path
    give us boldness to follow him
    who is the same Saviour
        yesterday, today and tomorrow.

(1) *A Lakota prayer from St Joseph's Indian School, South Dakota, USA.*
(2) *Adapted from a prayer used at Mengo Hospital, Uganda.*

Bless our voyage

O Lord, grant us a calm lake,
   little wind,
   little rain,
so that the canoes may proceed well,
so that they may proceed speedily.

Listen, O Lord

Listen, O Lord of the meeting rivers,
   things standing shall fall;
but the moving ever shall stay.

(1) *Anonymous prayer from Tanzania.*
(2) *Prayer of* BASAVANNA, *a medieval saint of South India.*

Keep your servants safe

O Christ, who are the way and the truth,
send now your guardian angel to go with your
      servants,
as once you did send him to Tobias,
and for your glory keep them safe and sound
    from all harm and evil.

Defend them from evil

O Saviour who did journey with Luke and Cleopas
    to Emmaus,
journey with your servants who now prepare to
    travel,
    defending them from every evil happening,
for you, who alone love mankind, are Almighty.

Pilgrim prayers of the Eastern Orthodox Church.

To tread a pilgrim's path

Teach us, O God,
  to view our life here on earth
  as a pilgrim's path to heaven,
and give us grace to tread it courageously
  in the company of your faithful people.
Help us to set our affections
  on the things above,
  not on the passing vanities of this world;
and grant that as we journey on
  in the way of holiness
  we may bear a good witness to our Lord,
and serve all who need our help
  along the way,
  for the glory of your name.

FRANK COLQUHOUN, *b. 1909, was a Canon Residentiary of Southwark and later Vice-Dean of Norwich; he is a considerable writer and collector of prayers.*

Guide me, O thou great Redeemer

Guide me, O thou great Redeemer,
   Pilgrim through this barren land;
I am weak, but thou art mighty;
   Hold me with thy powerful hand:
     Bread of heaven,
Feed me now and evermore.

Open now the crystal fountain
   Whence the healing stream doth flow;
Let the fiery cloudy pillar
   Lead me all my journey through:
     Strong deliverer,
Be thou still my strength and shield.

When I tread the verge of Jordan,
   Bid my anxious fears subside;
Death of death, and hell's destruction,
   Land me safe on Canaan's side:
     Songs and praises
I will ever give to thee.

WILLIAM WILLIAMS 1717–91, itinerant preacher who did not proceed beyond the diaconate. The hymn was translated from the Welsh by Peter and William Williams, and is usually sung to the rousing tune known as 'Cwm Rhondda'.

Teach us, your servants and pilgrims

Teach us, your servants and pilgrims,
        O King of Kings,
To walk trustfully in your presence
        and obey your majesty;
That, while we journey to the heavenly country,
Your voice may encourage,
        your arm protect,
        and your love transfigure us;
Through Jesus Christ our Lord.

ERIC MILNER-WHITE *1884–1963, Dean of York from 1941 to 1963, was a noted composer and collector of prayers. This prayer comes from* Daily Prayer.

To closely walk with thee to heaven

Forth in thy name, O Lord, I go,
   My daily labour to pursue;
Thee, only thee, resolved to know,
   In all I think, or speak or do.

The task thy wisdom hath assigned
   O let me cheerfully fulfil;
In all my works thy presence find,
   And prove thy good and perfect will.

Thee may I set at my right hand,
   Whose eyes my inmost substance see,
And labour on at thy command,
   And offer all my works to thee.

Give me to bear thy easy yoke,
   And every moment watch and pray,
And still to things eternal look,
   And hasten to thy glorious day;

For thee delightfully employ
   Whate'er thy bounteous grace hath given,
And run my course with even joy,
   And closely walk with thee to heaven.

CHARLES WESLEY *1707–88, preacher and hymn writer, brother to John Wesley.*

He leads me

The Lord's my shepherd, I'll not want;
    He makes me down to lie
In pastures green; he leadeth me
    The quiet waters by.

My soul he doth restore again,
    And me to walk doth make
Within the paths of righteousness,
    E'en for his own name's sake.

Yea, though I walk in death's dark vale,
    Yet will I fear no ill:
For thou art with me, and thy rod
    And staff me comfort still.

My table thou hast furnishèd
    In presence of my foes;
My head thou dost with oil anoint
    And my cup overflows.

Goodness and mercy all my life
    Shall surely follow me;
And in God's house for evermore
    My dwelling-place shall be.

Psalm 23, from the Scottish Psalter *1650.*

To be a pilgrim

Who would true valour see,
  Let him come hither;
One here will constant be,
  Come wind, come weather;
There's no discouragement
Shall make him once relent
His first avowed intent
    To be a pilgrim.

Whoso beset him round
  With dismal stories,
Do but themselves confound;
  His strength the more is.
No lion can him fright;
He'll with a giant fight,
But he will have a right
    To be a pilgrim.

Hobgoblin nor foul fiend
  Can daunt his spirit;
He knows he at the end
  Shall life inherit.
Then, fancies, fly away;
He'll not fear what men say;
He'll labour night and day
    To be a pilgrim.

JOHN BUNYAN 1628–88, was famous as a writer and preacher. This hymn comes from The Pilgrim's Progress from this World to That which is to come which he wrote in the 1670s, largely in prison. The imagery of life seen as a pilgrimage was used in several of his other works in which he was fearless in the pursuit of his own ideas, in spite of persecution.

Thou art the journey and the journey's end

O Father, give the spirit power to climb
To the fountain of all light, and be purified.
Break through the mists of earth, the weight of the
    clod,
Shine forth in splendour, thou that art calm
    weather,
And quiet resting place for faithful souls.
To see thee is the end and the beginning,
Thou carriest us, and thou dost go before,
Thou art the journey, and the journey's end.

BOETHIUS c. 480–524, born in Rome, was a statesman and philosopher who became an influence on the formation of mediaeval thought.

Light of the lonely pilgrim's heart

Light of the lonely pilgrim's heart,
   Star of the coming day,
Arise, and with thy morning beams
   Chase all our griefs away.

Come, blessèd Lord, bid every shore
   And answering island sing
The praises of thy royal name,
   And own thee as their King.

Bid the whole world, responsive now
   To the bright world above,
Break forth in rapturous strains of joy
   In answer to thy love.

Jesus, thy fair creation groans –
   The air, the earth, the sea –
In unison with all our hearts,
   And calls aloud for thee.

Thine was the Cross, with all its fruits
   Of grace and peace divine:
Be thine the crown of glory now,
   The palm of victory thine.

SIR EDWARD DENNY *1796–?* was *a founder member of the Plymouth Brethren and contributed to their hymnody.*

Safe within thy hand

Alone with none but thee, my God,
  I journey on my way:
What need I fear when thou art near,
  O King of night and day?
More safe am I within thy hand
Than if a host should round me stand.

My destined time is known to thee,
  And death will keep his hour;
Did warriors strong around me throng,
  They could not stay his power:
No walls of stone can man defend
When thou thy messenger dost send.

My life I yield to thy decree,
  And bow to thy control
In peaceful calm, for from thine arm
  No power can wrest my soul:
Could earthly omens e'er appal
A man that heeds the heavenly call?

The child of God can fear no ill,
  His chosen, dread no foe;
We leave our fate with thee, and wait
  Thy bidding when to go:
'Tis not from chance our comfort springs,
Thou art our trust, O King of kings.

ST COLUMBA 521–597, *the Irish missionary who established
himself on the Island of Iona in 563, is believed to have written the
original version of this hymn.*

Pilgrim way

Control me, O my God,
   gently, pervasively, irresistibly, increasingly;
so that I walk my pilgrim way
   steadily, and in a sure light;
so that I neither dally nor disobey,
   nor slip aside, nor stand still, nor sink down.
Control me, O God,
   by the pulse of your Presence,
     by your brightness about me;
by the spur of spiritual longing
     after your holy praise,
     after the image of your Son;
so that I move onward and upward with a song,
     and melody in my heart.
Then, O my God, change control into grasp,
   lest I ever deny my truest will,
   so that I cannot escape or fall away,
and the world pull back the pilgrim
     and steal his glory.

O Lord, let your arm grip me, lift me,
     land me safe home.
Bring me to Jerusalem that is yours,
   and set me with your blessed ones,
     with the princes of your people;
     the way ended, the peace unending,
     the perfect and pure for ever imperishable,
     and YOU all in all.

ERIC MILNER-WHITE *1884–1963. See note on page 15. This prayer is taken from* My God, My Glory.

Following the Master

Though my path repels my nature,
  And against each wish of mine,
Yet I'll meet what comes serenely,
  Strengthened by thy face divine;
Counting the cross a crown, when lifted,
  In afflictions, live in bliss:
A way of woes becomes the shortest
  Path to where the city is.

Weary pilgrim tossed by tempests,
  Raise thy gaze and now behold
Christ as active Mediator
  In long robes of charm untold;
Golden girdle of true friendship –
  On his train, a sound of bells
Ringing forth a full forgiveness,
  For in Him all mercy dwells.

ANN GRIFFITHS 1776–1805 spent all her short life at Dolwar Fechan in Dolanog, a small village in Montgomeryshire. Influenced by Calvinistic Methodism, which was powerful in the Wales of her day, she began to write hymns in the Welsh language which reflected her understanding of the Incarnation and knowledge of the Bible. She died the year after her marriage, two weeks after giving birth to a child. This hymn was translated by R. R. Williams.

Let me see thy foot-marks

O Jesus, I have promised
  To serve thee to the end;
Be thou for ever near me,
  My Master and my Friend:
I shall not fear the battle
  If thou art by my side,
Nor wander from the pathway
  If thou wilt be my guide.

O let me feel thee near me:
  The world is ever near;
I see the sights that dazzle,
  The tempting sounds I hear;
My foes are ever near me,
  Around me and within;
But, Jesus, draw thou nearer,
  And shield my soul from sin.

O let me hear thee speaking
  In accents clear and still,
Above the storms of passion,
  The murmurs of self-will;
O speak to reassure me,
  To hasten or control;
O speak, and make me listen,
  Thou guardian of my soul.

O Jesus, thou hast promised
  To all who follow thee,
That where thou art in glory
  There shall thy servant be;
And, Jesus, I have promised
  To serve thee to the end:

O give me grace to follow,
   My Master and my Friend.

O let me see thy foot-marks,
   And in them plant mine own;
My hope to follow duly
   Is in thy strength alone:
O guide me, call me, draw me,
   Uphold me to the end;
And then in heaven receive me,
   My Saviour and my Friend.

J. E. BODE *1816–74 was Rector of Westwell, Oxfordshire, one time tutor at Christ Church, Oxford and Bampton Lecturer.*

The Way, the Truth and the Life

O Lord Jesus Christ,
  the maker and redeemer of mankind, who have
      said,
    that you are the way, the truth and the life;
  the way, by doctrine, precepts, and examples;
  the truth, in promises;
  and the life, in reward;
I beseech you for your unspeakable love's sake,
  through which you have vouchsafed to employ
      yourself
    wholly in your saving of us,
  suffer me not at any time
    to stray from you,
    who are the way;
  nor to distrust your promises,
    who are the truth,
  and perform whatever you promise;
nor to rest in anything other than you,
    who are the way,
  beyond which there is nothing to be desired,
    neither in heaven, nor in earth.
By you we have learned the sure and ready way
    to true salvation,
  to the intent we should not wander any longer
    up and down the mazes of this world.
You have taught us thoroughly what to believe,
    what to do,
    what to hope,
    and wherein to rest.

DESIDERIUS ERASMUS c. 1466–1536, *a scholar of deep erudi-
tion and considerable intellect whose ideas paved the way for the
Reformation.*

Help me to follow

Lord Jesus Christ,
alive and at large in the world,
help me to follow and find you there today,
in the places where I work,
    meet people,
    spend money,
    and make plans.
Take me as a disciple of your kingdom,
to see through your eyes,
and hear the questions you are asking,
to welcome all others with your trust and truth,
and to change the things that contradict God's love,
by the power of the cross
and the freedom of your Spirit.

JOHN VERNON TAYLOR, b. 1914. After years as a missionary in
Africa and General Secretary of the Church Missionary Society
from 1963 to 1974, he became Bishop of Winchester until 1985.
This prayer comes from his book A Matter of Life and Death.

No resting place

Have faith in God, my heart,
　　trust and be unafraid;
God will fulfil in every part
　　each promise he has made.

Have faith in God, my mind,
　　though oft your light burns low;
God's mercy holds a wiser plan
　　than you can fully know.

Have faith in God, my soul,
　　his Cross for ever stands;
And neither life nor death can pluck
　　his children from his hands.

Lord Jesus, make me whole;
　　grant me no resting place,
Until I rest, heart, mind, and soul,
　　the captive of your grace.

Wherever I go, there God is

There is no place
Where God is not;
Wherever I go, there God is.
Now and always He upholds
Me with His power,
And keeps me safe in
His Love.

(1) B. A. REES, *b. 1911.*
(2) *Anon.*

Nearly overcome by weariness

Lord,
just as a pilgrim who travels all day
without eating or drinking
is nearly overcome by weariness,
but at last comes upon a good inn
and is well refreshed with food and drink,
so in the spiritual life
my soul wishes to renounce the love of the world
and love you, my God.
So I set myself to this,
but sometimes I pray and labour
in body and soul all day long
without feeling any comfort and joy.
Yet, Lord, you have pity on all your creatures
and you send me spiritual food
and comfort me with devotion as you see fit,
lest I perish, lose heart
or fall into depression and complaint.

WALTER HILTON *d. 1395 was one of the English mystics of the
fourteenth century. His* Ladder of Perfection, *on the gift of contem-
plation, upon which this extract is based, is one of his best known
works.*

The road ahead

My Lord God,
I have no idea where I am going.
I do not see the road ahead of me.
I cannot know for certain where it will end.
Nor do I really know myself,
and the fact that I think that I am following your
   will
does not mean that I am actually doing so.
But I believe that the desire to please you
does in fact please you.
And I hope I have that desire
   in all that I am doing.
I hope that I will never do anything
   apart from that desire.
And to know that if I do this,
you will lead me by the right road
though I may know nothing about it.
Therefore will I trust you always
though I may seem lost in the shadow of death.
I will not fear, for you are ever with me,
and you will never leave me
   to face my perils alone.

THOMAS MERTON *1915–68 was a Cistercion monk who be-
came a prolific spiritual writer. During the latter part of his life he
developed an interest in Eastern religions.*

Walking in faith

Through the dark night I wander on alone,
And, as one blinded, grope my weary way,
Without a lamp to shed its guiding ray;
I wander on unseen and seeing none,
And caring to behold but only One.

I see not, yet my heart will give me light,
And safer than the noonday sun will guide
To where the Bridegroom waiteth for the Bride;
So walking on in faith and not by sight
I cannot fear but he will guide me right.

AUGUSTA DRANE *1823–94 became a Roman Catholic as a young woman and later entered the Congregation of Dominican Sisters of St Catherine of Siena at Stone; she became Prioress Provincial with the name of Mother Francis Raphael, OSD.*

Lead thou me on

Lead, kindly Light, amid the encircling
    gloom
      Lead thou me on!
The night is dark, and I am far from home –
      Lead thou me on!
Keep thou my feet; I do not ask to see
The distant scene – one step enough for me.

I was not ever thus, nor prayed that thou
      Shouldst lead me on.
I loved to choose and see my path, but now
      Lead thou me on!
I loved the garish day, and, spite of fears,
Pride ruled my will: remember not past
    years.

So long thy power hath blest me, sure it still
      Will lead me on,
O'er moor and fen, o'er crag and torrent, till
      The night is gone;
And with the morn those angel faces smile
Which I have loved long since, and lost
    awhile.

JOHN HENRY NEWMAN *1801–90 was a Fellow of Oriel College, Oxford and a leading Tractarian until he became a Roman Catholic in 1845. He wrote many works of great distinction and was made a Cardinal in 1879.*

Lead home my going forth

O creator past all telling,
you have appointed from the treasures
    of your wisdom
the hierarchies of angels,
disposing them in wondrous order
    above the bright heavens,
and have so beautifully set out all parts
    of the universe.
You we call the true fount of wisdom
and the noble origin of all things.
Be pleased to shed on the darkness of mind
    in which I was born,
The twofold beam of your light
and warmth to dispel my ignorance and sin.
You make eloquent the tongues of children.
Then instruct my speech and touch my lips
    with graciousness.
Make me keen to understand, quick to learn,
able to remember;
make me delicate to interpret and ready to speak.
Guide my going in and going forward,
lead home my going forth.
You are true God and true man,
and live for ever and ever.

ST THOMAS AQUINAS 1225–74, *Dominican philosopher and theologian.*

Thou alone dost steer my boat

Eternal and most glorious God,
suffer me not so to undervalue myself
  as to give away my soul,
  thy soul,
  thy dear and precious soul,
  for nothing;
and all the world is nothing,
  if the soul be given for it.
Preserve therefore my soul, O Lord,
  because it belongs to thee,
and preserve my body
  because it belongs to my soul.
Thou alone dost steer my boat
  through all its voyage,
but hast a more especial care of it,
  when it comes to a narrow current,
  or to a dangerous fall of waters.
Thou hast a care of the preservation of my body
  in all the ways of my life;
but, in the straits of death,
  open thine eyes wider,
  and enlarge thy providence towards me so far
  that no illness or agony may shake and benumb
    the soul.
Do thou so make my bed in all my sickness
  that, being used to thy hand,
  I may be content with any bed of thy making.

JOHN DONNE *1573–1631, poet and Dean of St Paul's from
1621–1631.*

The road to holiness

God does not want you to deny yourself *good* things.
  That is no road to holiness.
A true fast is to deny yourself *bad* things:
  keep his commandments,
  do what he says,
  reject evil thoughts and desires
the moment they enter your imagination.
Reject what is wrong
  and serve God with a simple, uncomplicated
    heart.
If you do that, you are fasting –
  fasting in a way that pleases the Lord.

Lord, help us to follow this road.

THE 'SHEPHERD' OF HERMAS. *The Syriac writings attributed to a second-century Christian slave, are referred to under this title; the probable date is between 140–155.*

The pilgrim's aiding

May God be with you in every pass,
Jesus be with you on every knoll,
Spirit be with you by water's roll,
    On headland, on ridge, and on grass;
Each sea and land, each moor and each mead,
Each eve's lying-down, each rising's morn,
In the wave-trough, or on foam-crest borne,
    Each step which your journey does lead.

Be thou a smooth way

Before me be thou a smooth way,
Above me be thou a star-guide,
Behind me O be thou keen-eyed,
For the day, this night, and for aye.

I weary and heavy am driv'n,
Lead me on to the angels' place;
'Twere time now I went for a space
To Christ's court and the peace of heav'n.

If only thou, God of life, give
Smooth peace for me, at my back near,
Be as star, as helmsman to steer,
From smooth rest till rising I live.

These traditional prayers from the Hebrides are taken from Poems of the Western Highlands, *edited by G. R. D. McLean.*

For those travelling from home

O Lord, we beseech you,
for those who are travelling from home;
grant them an angel of peace as their
   fellow-traveller,
that they may receive no hurt from any one,
that they may finish their voyage
and their travels in much cheerfulness.

ST SERAPION *d. after 360, Bishop of Thmuis in the Nile delta from about 330; he was a close friend of St Athanasius and St Anthony.*

Comfort of the pilgrim soul

O Jesus,
Thou brightness of eternal glory,
Thou comfort of the pilgrim soul,
   with thee is my tongue without voice,
   and my very silence speaketh unto thee . . .
Come, O Come!
For without thee I shall have no joyful day
    nor hour;
   for thou art my joy,
   and without thee my table is empty . . .
Praise therefore and glory be unto thee,
O Wisdom of the Father;
   let my mouth,
   my soul,
   and all creatures together,
   praise and bless thee.

THOMAS À KEMPIS *1380–1471, an Augustinian Canon of Zwolle in the Netherlands in his book* The Imitation of Christ.

O happy band of pilgrims

O happy band of pilgrims,
   If onward ye will tread
With Jesus as your fellow
   To Jesus as your Head! . . .

The Cross that Jesus carried
   He carried as your due:
The Crown that Jesus weareth
   He weareth it for you.

The faith by which ye see him,
   The hope in which ye yearn,
The love that through all troubles
   To him alone will turn,

The trials that beset you,
   The sorrows ye endure,
The manifold temptations
   That death alone can cure,

What are they but his jewels
   Of right celestial worth?
What are they but the ladder
   Set up to heaven on earth?

O happy band of pilgrims,
   Look upward to the skies,
Where such a light affliction
   Shall win so great a prize.

JOHN MASON NEALE *1818–66, Anglican author and hymn writer, translated many works from Eastern Orthodox sources.*

The pathway of your will

O Christ our Master,
Give us a new confidence and deepen
    and increase our faith.
May we walk with our fellows not as those
    who have heard of you,
        but as those who are sure of you;
not as those who know *about* you,
        but as those who know you.
Then, timid though we have been,
    with many a glance behind us,
we shall walk bravely along the pathway
      of your will
      and all our fears will vanish.
Grant this, for your name's sake.

LESLIE WEATHERHEAD *1893–1976, preacher, writer and
healer. He was for many years minister of the City Temple,
London, and President of the Methodist Conference 1955–56.*

We seek thy perfect way

Thou God of truth and love,
    We seek thy perfect way,
Ready thy choice to approve,
    Thy providence to obey;
Enter into thy wise design,
    And sweetly lose our will in thine.

Why hast thou cast our lot
    In the same age and place,
And why together brought
    To see each other's face;
To join with living sympathy,
    And mix our friendly souls in thee?

Didst thou not make us one,
    That we might one remain,
Together travel on,
    And bear each other's pain;
Till all thy utmost goodness prove,
    And rise renewed in perfect love?

Then let us ever bear
    The blessed end in view,
And join with mutual care,
    To fight our passage through;
And kindly help each other on,
    Till all receive the starry crown.

CHARLES WESLEY *1707–88, preacher and hymn-writer, brother to John Wesley.*

Onward, therefore, pilgrim brothers

Through the night of doubt and sorrow
   Onward goes the pilgrim band,
Singing songs of expectation,
   Marching to the Promised Land.
Clear before us through the darkness
   Gleams and burns the guiding light;
Brother clasps the hand of brother,
   Stepping fearless through the night.

One the light of God's own presence
   O'er his ransomed people shed,
Chasing far the gloom and terror,
   Brightening all the path we tread:
One the object of our journey,
   One the faith which never tires,
One the earnest looking forward,
   One the hope our God inspires:

One the strain that lips of thousands
   Lift as from the heart of one:
One the conflict, one the peril,
   One the march in God begun:
One the gladness of rejoicing
   On the far eternal shore,
Where the one almighty Father
   Reigns in love for evermore.

BERNHARDT SEVERIN INGEMANN *1789–1862, Professor of Danish language, Academy of Soro, Denmark. Translated from the Danish by Sabine Baring-Gould 1834–1924, Rector of Lew Trenchard in Devon, writer and composer of hymns.*

The way that leads to heaven

O Lord, thy hands have formed us,
and thou has sent us into this world
that we may walk in the way that leads to heaven
    and thyself,
and may find a lasting rest in thee
who art the source and centre of our souls.
Look in pity on us poor pilgrims in the narrow way;
let us not go astray, but reach at last our true home
    where our Father dwells.
Guide and govern us from day to day,
and bestow on us food and strength
  for body and soul,
that we may journey on in peace.
Forgive us for having hitherto so often wavered
    or looked back,
and let us henceforward march straight on
    in the way of thy laws,
and may our last step be a safe
  and peaceful passage
    to the arms of thy love,
and the blessed fellowship of the saints in light.
Hear us, O Lord, and glorify thy name in us
that we may glorify thee for ever and ever.

GERHARD TERSTEEGEN 1697–1769, *German Protestant devotional writer who gave up his profession for solitude.*

Lead us, heavenly Father

Lead us, heavenly Father, lead us
   O'er the world's tempestuous sea;
Guard us, guide us, keep us, feed us,
   For we have no help but thee;
Yet possessing every blessing,
   If our God our Father be.

Saviour, breathe forgiveness o'er us:
   All our weakness thou dost know;
Thou didst tread this earth before us,
   Thou didst feel its keenest woe;
Lone and dreary, faint and weary,
   Through the desert thou didst go.

Spirit of our God, descending,
   Fill our hearts with heavenly joy,
Love with every passion blending,
   Pleasure that can never cloy:
Thus provided, pardoned, guided,
   Nothing can our peace destroy.

JAMES EDMESTON *1791–1867*. *An architect by profession and Independent by birth, he later joined the Church of England.*

Steer the vessel of our life

O Lord our God,
teach us, we beseech you,
to ask you aright for the right blessings.
Steer the vessel of our life toward yourself,
    tranquil haven of all storm-tossed souls.
Show us the course wherein we should go.
Renew a willing spirit within us.
Let your Spirit curb our wayward senses,
    and guide and enable us unto that
    which is our true good,
    to keep your laws,
and in all our works evermore to rejoice
in your glorious and gladdening presence.
For yours is the glory and praise
    from all your saints for ever and ever.

ST BASIL *c. 330–379, named 'the Great'. His writings and learning made him one of the most significant figures of the Eastern
Church. He became Bishop of Caesarea in 370.*

In our wanderings be our guide

Father, hear the prayer we offer:
  Not for ease that prayer shall be,
But for strength that we may ever
  Live our lives courageously.

Not for ever in green pastures
  Do we ask our way to be;
But the steep and rugged pathway
  May we tread rejoicingly.

Not for ever by still waters
  Would we idly rest and stay;
But would smite the living fountains
  From the rocks along our way.

Be our strength in hours of weakness,
  In our wanderings be our guide;
Through endeavour, failure, danger,
  Father, be thou at our side.

LOVE MARIA WILLIS *1824–1908, an American and wife of a doctor.*

Onward, Christians

Oft in danger, oft in woe,
Onward, Christians, onward go;
Bear the toil, maintain the strife,
Strengthened with the Bread of Life.

Onward, Christians, onward go,
Join the war, and face the foe;
Will ye flee in danger's hour?
Know ye not your Captain's power?

Let not sorrow dim your eye;
Soon shall every tear be dry:
Let not fears your course impede;
Great your strength, if great your need.

Let your drooping hearts be glad;
March in heavenly armour clad;
Fight, nor think the battle long:
Soon shall victory wake your song.

Onward then in battle move;
More than conquerors ye shall prove:
Though opposed by many a foe,
Christian soldiers, onward go.

HENRY KIRKE WHITE *1785–1806, poet and hymn writer who
died aged twenty-two while a student for the ministry.*

To choose again the pilgrim way

Now let us from this table rise,
  renewed in body, mind, and soul;
With Christ we die and live again,
  his selfless love has made us whole.

With minds alert, upheld by grace,
  to spread the Word in speech and deed,
We follow in the steps of Christ,
  at one with man in hope and need.

To fill each human house with love,
  it is the sacrament of care;
The work that Christ began to do
  we humbly pledge ourselves to share.

Then give us courage, Father God,
  to choose again the pilgrim way,
And help us to accept with joy
  the challenge of tomorrow's day.

FREDERICK KAAN, b. 1929. Born and educated in the Nether-lands, he was ordained to the Congregational ministry in Britain in 1955. He became a Provincial Moderator of the United Re-formed Church in 1968, after ten years of ecumenical ministry in Geneva.

The journey towards the city

May we all live in the peace
  that comes from you.
May we journey towards your city,
sailing through the waters of sin,
    untouched by the waves,
      borne tranquilly along by the Holy Spirit,
      your wisdom beyond all telling.
Night and day, until the last day of all,
      may our praises give you thanks,
      our thanksgiving praise you:
You who alone are both Father and Son,
      Son and Father,
        the Son who is our Tutor and our Teacher,
        together with the Holy Spirit.

CLEMENT OF ALEXANDRIA *c. 150–c. 215. Probably born in Athens, he became a theologian and moved to Egypt to be head of the Catechetical School at Alexandria.*

Wearied pilgrim

Never weather-beaten sail more willing bent to
     shore,
Never tired pilgrim's limbs affected slumber more,
  than my wearied spirit now longs to fly
       out of my troubled breast:
O come quickly, sweetest Lord, and take my soul to
     rest.

Ever blooming are the joys of heaven's high paradise,
Cold age deafs not there our ears, nor vapour dims
     our eyes;
Glory there the sun outshines;
  whose beams the blessèd only see;
O come quickly, glorious Lord, and raise my spirit to
     thee.

THOMAS CAMPION *1567–1620, poet, musician, doctor.*

To enter into that gate

Bring us, O Lord God,
at our last awakening into the house
      and gate of heaven,
to enter into that gate and dwell
      in that house,
where there shall be no darkness nor dazzling,
      but one equal light;
      no noise nor silence,
      but one equal music;
      no fears nor hopes,
      but one equal possession;
      no ends nor beginnings,
      but one equal eternity;
in the habitations of thy majesty and thy glory,
      world without end.

JOHN DONNE 1573–1631, see note on p. 34. This extract is taken
from a sermon preached on 29 February 1628.

Epitaph

Here down my wearied limbs I'll lay;
My pilgrim's staff; my weed of gray:
My palmer's hat; my scallop shell;
My cross; my cord; and all farewell.

ROBERT HERRICK *1591–1674* took orders in *1629* and was vicar of Dean Prior in Devonshire until he was ejected for royalist sympathies in *1647*. He was reinstated in his parish in *1662*, at the Restoration. He has been called the greatest of the Cavalier poets. This extract comes from a poem which he entitled 'On himselfe' and was included in a collection called Hesperides, published in *1648*.

PILGRIMAGE
TO SPECIAL PLACES

That pilgrimages continue to be made to the cathedrals of England is a consequence of their history. Many were built in honour of great figures of the past whose memories pilgrims wish to recapture and to hallow. But these buildings are more than the shrines of dead saints. The prayer that has been offered down the ages has given certain cathedrals an atmosphere of holiness which continues to draw pilgrims today to add their own prayers to God.

But sites which draw pilgrims are not necessarily large cathedrals. Some are outwardly small and insignificant buildings; some have hardly any buildings left standing; others, like Taizé in France and Medjugorje in Yugoslavia, are of recent date. Yet all possess an undoubtedly special quality, that is recognised, and contributed to, by the sensitive visitor on a journey of prayer and discovery.

CANTERBURY

Hallowed as the mother church of the Anglican heritage, this is the place where such Archbishops as Augustine, Dunstan, Anselm and Thomas Becket are remembered for the qualities which made them saints; and where, in the chapel of modern martyrs, the examples of the lives of Dietrich Bonhoeffer, Maximilian Kolbe, Martin Luther King and others are held up to the world.

Prayer of the Portsmouth Diocesan Pilgrimage 1983

We give thanks to God that
united as a company,
we have been led so far in safety.
Now we gather as the pilgrim people of God
to walk to the Cathedral Church of Christ.
Following the example of the children of Israel,
who before their journey through the wilderness
    to the promised land
escaped death by passing through the waters
    of the Red Sea,
so we who are baptised unto the death
    and resurrection of Christ
now renew our renunciation of all that is evil
and retrace the cross of Christ upon our foreheads.
In his strength alone we journey
until we come to behold the presence of God.

Collect of the Birmingham Diocesan Pilgrimage to Canterbury 1986

Heavenly Father, you have brought us to the place
where the Christian faith was rooted again;
to the shrine of martyrs and prophets;
to the throne of Archbishops;
to the home of scholars and saints;
and to the Mother Church of our
    Anglican Communion.
Lead us by your Spirit, in our pilgrimage
    to Canterbury,
and by that Spirit, kindle in our hearts
gratitude for the past, and hope for the years ahead;
through Jesus Christ our Lord.

Prayer at the Pontifical Mass to commemorate the 800th anniversary of the martyrdom of St Thomas Becket 1970

O God, who did translate blessed Thomas
your martyr and bishop,
from sufferings to joys;
concede, we beseech you,
that we who venerate his translation on earth,
may, by his patronage,
be translated to heaven,
through Christ our Lord.

Prayers on the 800th anniversary of the death of St Thomas Becket 1970

We offer Almighty God our praise and thanksgiving
for his martyr Saint Thomas,
and for the Cathedral Church in which he died;
and let us pray that Christian people

who are now divided
may learn to recognise one another
as disciples of the same Lord,
and in him rebuild the unity
of his Church.
May God's blessing be upon us all now
and in the days to come.

O Lord, who did give to your servant Saint Thomas
grace to lay aside the fear of man,
and to be faithful even to death:
Grant that we, unmindful of worldly honour,
may fight the wrong,
uphold your rule,
and serve you to our lives' end:
Through Jesus Christ, our Lord.

At the chapel of saints and martyrs of our own time

Throughout the centuries
men and women have given their lives
    for Christianity;
our own century is no exception.
Their deaths are in union
with the life-giving death of
    our Lord Jesus Christ
    the Saviour of mankind.

In this chapel
we thank God for the sacrifice of martyrdom
whereby truth is upheld
and God's providence enriched.
We pray that we may be
worthy of their sacrifice.

57

CHESTER

An important Roman city, Chester was rebuilt in the tenth century when a Christian church was established on the site of the present cathedral. A seventh-century abbess, St Werburgh, revered for her holy life, was re-buried here.

Pilgrim prayers used by the cathedral

Heavenly Father,
as we follow in the footsteps of our forefathers
on our pilgrimage of faith,
fill us with your heavenly grace
and so make us faithful witnesses to all people
of the love of Jesus.
Grant that we, being firmly grounded
in the truth of the Gospel,
may be faithful to its teaching,
both in word and deed,
through Christ our Lord.

Almighty God,
by whose grace Saint Werburgh,
kindled with the fire of your love,
became a burning and a shining light
     in the Church,
inflame us with the same spirit
     of discipline and love,
that we may ever walk before you
as children of Light,
through Jesus Christ our Lord.

CHICHESTER

The bishopric of Chichester was transferred here from Selsey in 1075, and the cathedral built in the twelfth and thirteenth centuries. Its most renowned bishop was the saintly Richard, consecrated in 1244, and canonised in 1262, nine years after his death.

Prayer of St Richard of Chichester

Thanks be to thee, my Lord Jesus Christ,
For all the benefits which thou hast given to me,
For all the pains and insults which thou hast
    borne for me.
O most merciful redeemer, friend and brother,
May I know thee more clearly,
Love thee more dearly,
And follow thee more nearly,
Day by day.

DURHAM

The first cathedral on this site was begun at the end of the tenth century, to house the bones of St Cuthbert (d. 687), brought to Durham from Lindisfarne. The present building dates from 1093. In addition to the tomb of Cuthbert, it also contains the bones of the Venerable Bede (c. 673–735) and so honours two of the greatest figures in the history of the Church in the north of England.

Collect for St Cuthbert's day–20 March

Almighty God,
who didst call thy servant Cuthbert
    from keeping sheep
to follow thy Son and to be a shepherd
    of thy people,
mercifully grant that we,
following his example and caring for
    those who are lost,
may bring them home to thy fold,
through thy Son Jesus Christ our Lord.

For St Cuthbert – 20 March

Lord, open our eyes to your presence,
Open our minds to your peace,
Open our lives to your power.
Then, guide us on our pilgrimage throughout life,
That with the memory of Cuthbert in our minds
And the example of Cuthbert for us to follow,

We may walk in the way of peace
And find our freedom in His service
Who is our Saviour, Jesus Christ.

David Adam

A prayer of the Venerable Bede

I pray thee, merciful Jesus,
that as thou hast graciously granted me
to drink down sweetly from the Word
which tells of thee,
so wilt thou kindly grant
that I may come at length to thee,
the fount of all wisdom,
and stand before thy face for ever.

For St Bede – 27 May

Father, we thank you for the Venerable Bede
    and his faith.
He knew your Son Jesus Christ
to be the Morning Star,
who, when the dark night of this world is past,
will bring us to be with you
in the Light of eternal day.
Help us to rejoice in this truth that he taught,
through the same Jesus Christ our Lord.

David Adam

DAVID ADAM b. 1936 is Vicar of Lindisfarne. He has made a
lifelong study of the early Celtic Church, and has written many
prayers in the Celtic tradition.

ELY

In the mid-seventh century, Etheldreda, daughter of Anna, a Christian king of the East Angles, made her way to Ely, then an island in the Fens, for a life of prayer. In 672 she became a nun and, as Abbess until her death, established a double monastery of monks and nuns. In 870 it was destroyed by Danes, but rebuilt in 970 by Benedictine monks. The present beautiful building was begun in 1082.

Prayers for pilgrims to Ely Cathedral

O God, who did bestow such grace upon
    our foundress Etheldreda,
that she gave herself wholly to the service
    of your true religion:
Mercifully grant that we who commemorate
    her faith and constancy,
may likewise serve you faithfully all our days,
and finally by your guiding may come
unto the glorious fellowship of your saints;
through Jesus Christ our Lord.

Grant, we beseech you, Almighty God,
that we who have our foundress, Saint Etheldreda,
    in thankful remembrance,
may come at the last to be partakers
    of her heavenly reward;
through Jesus Christ, your Son our Lord.

HEREFORD

The bishopric was founded in 676 and the main part of the present cathedral dates from 1097–1110. The most famous medieval bishop was Thomas Cantilupe (1275–82) who gained a reputation as a scholar as well as a wise and caring bishop who stood against evil in whatever guise it came. His shrine in the Lady Chapel was second only to that of Thomas Becket at Canterbury for pilgrims.

Prayers for pilgrims to Hereford Cathedral

O Lord Christ, true Light of mankind,
let your love burn always in my heart,
and in the hearts of all for whom I pray.
Make every one of us a light in the world
for you.

Christ our Saviour,
Shed your light upon the earth I have to tread,
that I may keep to it without stumbling,
and without faltering,
and come in the end to see you face to face
in your heavenly kingdom.

Almighty God,
glorified in all your saints,
who gave grace to your servant Thomas Cantilupe
steadfastly to resist evil and uphold justice:
grant us who commemorate his holy life
likewise to live blamelessly
that we may win with him an eternal crown;
through our Lord and Saviour Jesus Christ.

LICHFIELD

The see of the ancient kingdom of Mercia, Lichfield's most famed bishop was St Chad, trained by St Aidan at Lindisfarne and installed in 669. The present cathedral dates mainly from the thirteenth century.

Prayers for the use of pilgrims to Lichfield Cathedral

Almighty God, our heavenly Father,
by whose providence
thy blessed servant Chad
was sent here to be bishop of thy Church,
grant that we who have entered into
the spiritual heritage which he left in this place,
may like him be inspired
to devote ourselves wholly to thy service;
and ever to maintain
the virtue of love and peace
one to another, and towards all the faithful;
through the grace of Him who is the prince of peace,
our Lord and Saviour Jesus Christ.

Bless, O Lord,
the work and worship of this Cathedral Church,
dedicated to the name of thy blessed Mother, Mary,
and thy holy bishop, Chad,
and grant that this house,
built gloriously to thee,
may kindle in the hearts of those who enter therein,
a spirit of love, reverence and faith,
through Jesus Christ our Lord.

A prayer of Dr Samuel Johnson, written on his birthday, 18 September 1758

Almighty and most merciful Father,
who yet sparest and yet supportest me,
who supportest me in my weakness,
and sparest me in my sins,
and hast now granted to me to begin another year;
enable me to improve the time which is set before
  me
to thy glory and my own salvation.
Impress upon my soul such repentance
of the days misspent in idleness and folly,
that I may henceforth diligently attend
to the business of my station in the world,
and to all the duties which thou has commanded.
Let thy Holy Spirit comfort and guide me,
that in my passage through the pains or pleasures
of the present state,
I may never be tempted to forgetfulness of thee.
Let my life be useful, and my death be happy;
let me live according to thy laws,
and die with just confidence in thy mercy,
for the sake of Jesus Christ our Lord.

SAMUEL JOHNSON *1709–84, man of letters and lexicographer, was Lichfield's most famous son. Included among his considerable literary output were many prayers.*

LINCOLN

A see was established here by Bishop Remigius (died 1092) and during medieval times it was the biggest diocese in England, stretching from the Thames to the Humber. The fine cathedral dates from 1086 and was largely completed before 1300. St Hugh (1186–1200) was its most famous bishop.

Prayer of St Hugh

Help us, Lord,
with whatever we own,
    whatever we do,
    whatever we are,
to make a loving response
to your great love,
Maker, Redeemer, Sustainer of all.

Collect for St Hugh's Day – November 17

O merciful Father,
who did endow your servant Hugh of Lincoln
with a wise and cheerful boldness
and taught him to commend the discipline
    of a holy life
    to kings and princes;
Give us grace like him not only to be bold,
but to have just cause for boldness,
even the fear and love of yourself alone:
through Jesus Christ our Lord. Amen.

ST DAVID'S

Originally the site of a monastery on the South Wales coast, the cathedral was one of the great centres of Celtic Christianity. St David, who lived in the sixth century, builder of monasteries and patron saint of Wales, is buried and honoured here, amid beautiful surroundings.

Prayers for pilgrims to St David's

O God, who by the teaching
of thy blessed servant Saint David,
didst cause the light of the Gospel
to shine in the land of Wales;
grant, we beseech thee,
that having his life and labours
in remembrance,
we may show forth our thankfulness
unto thee for the same,
by following the example of his most holy life.
through Jesus Christ our Lord.

O Lord Jesus Christ,
who didst charge thine apostles
to preach the gospel to every creature:
prosper, we pray thee,
the work of thy Church in this land.
Give vision and courage to our bishops
and all who exercise spiritual leadership;
and so inflame the hearts of thy people with burning
  love
that they may be moved to share with others

the blessing of thy redeeming love;
who livest and reignest with the Father
and the Holy Spirit,
one God, for ever and ever. Amen.

WINCHESTER

The diocese of Winchester was established in the seventh century, and the present cathedral buildings were begun in 1093. St Swithun, its bishop from 852–62, and adviser to Egbert, King of Wessex, brought fame to the diocese and is buried here.

Collect for St Swithun's day – 15 July

Almighty God, by whose grace
we celebrate again the feast day
of your faithful servant Swithun;
grant that, as he governed with gentleness
the people committed to his care,
so we, entering with gladness
into a rich inheritance,
may always seek to build up your Church
in unity and love;
through Jesus Christ our Lord,
who is alive and reigns with you
and the Holy Spirit,
one God, now and for ever.

An important Roman town, York had a bishop as early as 314 and became an archbishopric in 735. Within the cathedral, commonly called the Minster, saints connected with the foundation are commemorated: Paulinus, Edwin, and the Abbess Hilda of Whitby; also St William of York (d. 1154), a medieval Archbishop. The fine present building, dating from the mid-thirteenth century, is one of the most popular with modern pilgrims.

Prayer used in pilgrimage processions

O Lord Christ, Lamb of God, Lord of Lords,
call us, who are called to be saints,
   along the way of thy Cross;
draw us, who would draw nearer our King,
   to the foot of thy Cross;
cleanse us, who are not worthy to approach,
   with the pardon of thy Cross;
instruct us, the ignorant and blind,
   in the school of thy Cross;
arm us, for the battles of holiness,
   by the might of thy Cross;
bring us, in the fellowship of thy sufferings,
   to the victory of thy Cross;
and seal us in the kingdom of thy glory
   among the servants of thy Cross,
O crucified Lord;
who with the Father and the Holy Ghost
livest and reignest
one God, almighty, eternal,
world without end.

Prayer at the nave altar

Grant us, Lord,
in thought, faith;
in word, wisdom;
in deed, courage;
in life, service;
through Jesus Christ our Lord.

GLASTONBURY

This small town in Somerset is the site of one of the oldest centres of human habitation in England; histories and legends have grown up which associate King Arthur and his queen with this place; also Joseph of Arimathea. Blake may have had this in mind when he wrote his poem 'Jerusalem'. A large abbey flourished here from earliest Christian times and the great Dunstan *c.* 909–88, later Archbishop of Canterbury, was Abbot 943–57.

Glastonbury prayer

Father of all,
in ancient time
your Son's disciples planted
the staff of faith in Glastonbury.
Here we have journeyed to give thanks,
that through her many saints,
that faith flowered, and brought forth
a mighty abbey.
We remember all those who down the years
prayed here in Jesus' name,
taught here the truth of his gospel,
built here to your great glory,
worked here to advance your kingdom,
suffered here for their faith in you.

Bless us and all who come on pilgrimage
to Glastonbury.
Guide our feet on the path of righteousness;

inspire us by your Spirit
to lead others into your Way.
Protect us from all evil.
And restore in us the vision of your Jerusalem.

IONA

This island to the west of Mull in the Western Islands of Scotland has an ancient Christian tradition; here St Columba came from Ireland in 563, and founded a monastery which became a centre of Celtic Christianity. In more recent times the Church of Scotland formed the Iona Community, under the leadership of the Revd George (later Lord) Macleod, in 1938.

Prayer attributed to St Columba

That I might bless the Lord
Who conserves all;
Heaven with its countless bright orders,
Land, strand and flood;
That I might search the books all
That would be good for my soul;
At times kneeling to beloved heaven;
At times at psalm singing;
At times contemplating the king of heaven,
Holy the chief;
At times at work without compulsion;
This would be delightful.
At times picking kelp from the rocks;
At times at fishing;
At times giving food to the poor;
At times in a solitary cell,
The best advice to me has been granted.

Prayer used by the Iona Community at the beginning of each weekly pilgrimage around the island

Bless to me, O God, the earth beneath my feet,
Bless to me, O God, the path whereon I go,
Bless to me, O God, the people whom I meet,
Today, tonight and tomorrow. Amen.

LINDISFARNE

Popularly known as Holy Island, it is noted for its associations with the seventh-century saints Aidan and Cuthbert. Famed as a missionary centre and as a monastic school, it was also a bishopric until the see was transferred to Durham in 995.

Ancient prayer attributed to St Aidan, prayed daily at Marygate House retreat centre

Lord, this bare island,
make it thy place of peace.
Here be the peace
of brothers serving men.
Here be the peace
of holy rules obeying.
Here be the peace
of praise by dark or day.
Be this island
thy holy island.
I, Lord, thy servant Aidan,
speak this prayer.
Be it in thy care.

Prayer for St Aidan's day – 31 August

We thank you, Father,
For Jesus, the Light in our darkness;
and for Saint Aidan,
a light in the Dark Ages.
We thank you for the light
that has streamed from this Holy Island,

reaching throughout our land
and to other parts of the world.
Help us, Lord, in our time
to pass on this light,
Through him who is the Light of the World,
Jesus Christ.

David Adam

Prayer for the Holy Island of Lindisfarne

Lord, your presence fills this island.
Your presence is peace.
Peace to all who live here.
Peace to all who visit here.
Peace in this holy place.
Peace to pilgrim and seeker.
Peace to the troubled and lost.
Peace by day and by night.
Peace in dark and in light.
Lord, your presence fills our lives.
Your presence is peace.

David Adam

LITTLE GIDDING

In 1625 Nicholas Ferrar established in this Hunting-don village a lay religious community within the tradition of the Church of England. A household of about thirty people lived under a rule of prayer, worship and charitable works. The community was destroyed by a Puritan raid in 1646, but has been revived in the present century as the Community of Christ the Sower. T. S. Eliot immortalised the spirit of Little Gidding in his poem of that name.

Undertakings made by the modern Community

We commit ourselves to one another as
    fellow-disciples of Christ,
worshipping him together in prayer and in action.

We offer all that we have to be used in his service,
asking that we may each receive according to our
    needs.

We seek to live in harmony with one another,
bearing witness to the peace to which all people are
    called.

We strive to order our lives in obedience to God's
    will,
supporting one another in our various vocations.

Lines from 'Little Gidding' I

> . . . If you came this way,
> Taking any route, starting from anywhere,
> At any time or at any season,
> It would always be the same: you would have to put
>   off
> Sense and notion. You are not here to verify,
> Instruct yourself, or inform curiosity
> Or carry report. You are here to kneel
> Where prayer has been valid. And prayer is more
> Than an order of words, the conscious occupation
> Of the praying mind, or the sound of the voice
>   praying.
> And what the dead had no speech for, when living,
> They can tell you, being dead: the communication
> Of the dead is tongued with fire beyond the language
>   of the living.
> Here, the intersection of the timeless moment
> Is England and nowhere. Never and always

T. S. Eliot

THOMAS STEARNS ELIOT *1888–1965, American born poet and critic who joined the Church of England, winner of the Nobel Prize for Literature 1948.*

NORWICH – ST JULIAN'S

In the mid-fourteenth century, Julian, a young woman probably in her twenties, became an anchorite attached to a church in Norwich. On 8 May 1373 she received a series of visions or 'showings' in which she experienced a sight of the Passion of Jesus, and the book she wrote later, *Revelations of Divine Love*, has become a classic with its simple profundity. St Julian's church has become a place of pilgrimage for the many people who are attracted by her writings.

Collect used at St Julian's church

Most Holy Lord,
the ground of our beseeching,
who through your servant Julian
revealed the wonder of your love:
grant that as we are created in your nature
and restored by your grace,
our wills may be so made one with yours
that we may come to see you
face to face
and gaze on you for ever.

Prayer based on words of Julian of Norwich

Lord, you are God.
Lord, you are in all things.
Lord, you do all things.
You never remove your hands
   from your works,
nor ever will, without end.

You guide all things
to the end that you ordained them for,
   before time began,
with the same power
and wisdom and love
   with which you made them;
how could anything be amiss?

WALSINGHAM

In the eleventh century the Lady Richeldis, of Walsingham in Norfolk, received a vision of the Blessed Virgin Mary, in which she was instructed to build a chapel after the model of the home of the Holy Family in Nazareth, in honour of the Incarnation. Pilgrims flocked to the shrine from all over Europe until it was suppressed at the Reformation. Revived in 1922, it is now one of the most important pilgrimage centres in the Church of England. There is also a Roman Catholic shrine, giving it an ecumenical dimension.

Prayers for use by pilgrims to Walsingham

We beseech you, O Lord,
to pour your grace into our hearts;
that, as we know the Incarnation of your Son
Jesus Christ,
by the message of an angel,
so by his cross and passion
we may be brought
unto the glory of his resurrection;
through the same
Jesus Christ our Lord.

O God, in your kindness
and in your desire
that all men should be
reconciled to you,
you offer us
this special time of pilgrimage
that we may acknowledge you

as our Creator and Father.
Help us during these days
so that we may dedicate ourselves
to do your will,
which is to restore
all things in Christ,
who lives and reigns for ever and ever.

A pilgrim's prayer to Our Lady of Walsingham

O Gracyous lady, glory of Jerusalem,
Cypresse of Syon and joye of Israle,
Rose of Jeryco and Sterre of Bethleem:
O gloryous lady, our askynge nat repell;
In mercy all wymen ever thou dost excell.
Therefore blessed lady graunt thou thy great grace
To all that thee devoutly visyte in this place.

'A Pilgrim's Prayer to Our Lady of Walsingham' by an unknown composer, was published about 1495 by Richard Pynson, King's Printer to Henry VII, who introduced roman type into England.

WESTMINSTER ABBEY

London's most famous church, the Collegiate Church of St Peter is not a cathedral, but a 'Royal Peculiar', the site of the burial place of several kings and queens, and of many of the nation's heroes.

To Your Glory

O everlasting God,
with whom a thousand years are but one day,
and in whose name are treasured here
   the memorials of many generations;
grant to those who labour in this place
such measures of your grace and wisdom,
that they may neglect no portion
   of their manifold inheritance,
but so guard and use it to your glory
and the enlargement of your Church,
that the consecration of all human powers
may set forward your purpose
of gathering up into one all things in Christ;
through whom to you be glory,
now and evermore.

John Armitage Robinson

JOHN ARMITAGE ROBINSON *1858–1933 was Dean of Westminster from 1902 to 1911.*

ASSISI

The hill town of Assisi in northern Italy was the birthplace of two remarkable saints at the turn of the twelfth/thirteenth centuries: St Francis, founder of the Franciscan Order, and St Clare, through his influence founder of the Poor Clares. Their generosity of spirit, compassion for the poor, and love of nature has endeared them to subsequent generations who have travelled to Assisi to honour them and to seek to follow in their footsteps.

Prayers of St Francis

Let every creature
  in heaven, on earth
  in the sea and in the depths,
give praise,
  glory, honour and blessing
to him
  who suffered so much for us,
  who has given so many good things,
  and who will continue to do so for the future.
For he is our power and strength,
  he who alone is good
  who is most high,
  who is all-powerful, admirable and glorious;
  who alone is holy, praiseworthy, and blessed
  throughout endless ages.

Almighty, eternal, just and merciful God,
grant us in our misery the grace
　　to do for you alone
　　　　what we know you want us to do,
　　　　and always
　　to desire what pleases you.
Thus,
　　　　inwardly cleansed,
　　　　interiorly enlightened,
　　　　and inflamed by the fire of the Holy Spirit,
may we be able to follow
　　in the footprints of your beloved Son,
　　our Lord Jesus Christ.
And,
by your grace alone,
may we make our way to You,
　　Most High,
　　who live and rule
　　in perfect Trinity and simple Unity,
and are glorified,
　　God all-powerful
　　for ever and ever.

Prayer of St Francis before the crucifix

Most high, glorious God,
enlighten the darkness of my heart,
and give me, Lord,
　　a correct faith,
　　a certain hope,
　　perfect charity,
　　sense and knowledge,
so that I may carry out
your holy and true command.

From St Francis' 'Office of the Passion'

Offer up your bodies and take up his holy cross
and follow his most holy commands even to the end.

Prayer of St Clare

O blessed poverty,
   who bestows eternal riches on those
   who love and embrace her,

O holy poverty,
   to those who possess and desire you
   God promises the kingdom of heaven
   and offers, indeed, eternal glory and blessed life.

O God-centred poverty,
   whom the Lord Jesus Christ
   who ruled and now rules heaven and earth,
   who spoke and things were made,
condescended to embrace before all else.

BEC

The Benedictine abbey of Bec near Rouen in Normandy was founded in 1041. It soon established a great reputation as a place of piety and learning and many of its most gifted monks were absorbed into the Church in England: three became Archbishops of Canterbury, Lanfranc, Anselm and Theobald. Bec's generosity led to its own decline, but in recent times the Abbey has come into new life and links have been forged with the Church of England in particular.

Prayer from St Anselm, 'Proslogion', written between 1170 and 1180

My God,
    I pray that I may so know you and love you
    that I may rejoice in you.
And if I may not do so fully in this life,
    let me go steadily on
to the day when I come to that fullness.
Let the knowledge of you increase in me here,
    and there let it come to its fullness.
Let your love grow in me here,
    and there let it be fulfilled,
so that here my joy may be in a great hope,
    and there in full reality.
Lord,
    you have commanded, or rather advised us,
      to ask by your Son
and you have promised that we shall receive,
    'that our joy may be full'.

That which you counsel
through our 'wonderful counsellor'
is what I am asking for, Lord.
Let me receive
that which you promised through your truth,
'that my joy may be full'.
God of truth,
I ask that I may receive,
so that my joy may be full.
Meanwhile, let my mind meditate on it,
let my tongue speak of it,
let my heart love it,
let my mouth preach it,
let my soul hunger for it,
my flesh thirst for it,
and my whole being desire it
until I enter into the joy of my Lord,
who is God one and triune, blessed forever.

Translated by Benedicta Ward SLG

BENEDICTA WARD *is a member of the Anglican religious community of the Sisters of the Love of God. She teaches theology and medieval history at Oxford University.*

COMPOSTELA

From the tenth to the sixteenth century Santiago de
Compostela in Spain was one of the most popular
places of pilgrimage in Europe. Images of St James the
Great still bear the pilgrims' hat and scallop shell
associated with Compostela, where his bones were
alleged to have been brought. *'Les chemins de Saint
Jacques'* were as well known as the roads to Rome,
and nowadays Compostela enshrines the hopes of
Europeans for a unity and peace that transcend
national boundaries.

Prayer of Pope John Paul II

May all who come to Santiago de Compostela,
following in the footsteps of Christian pilgrims from
many different times and places, be renewed in
the faith which comes to us from the apostles; in
union with the whole Church may they commit
themselves generously to follow Jesus Christ, who
alone is the Way, the Truth and the Life.

From The Santiago de Compostela
Declaration of the Council of Europe

May the faith which has inspired pilgrims
throughout history, uniting them in a common
aspiration and transcending national differences and
interests, inspire us today . . . to travel along these
routes in order to build a society founded on
tolerance, respect for others, freedom and solidarity.

Collect for St James the Apostle – 25 July

Merciful God,
we pray that as your holy apostle St James
left his father and all that he had
and obeyed the calling
   of your Son Jesus Christ even to death:
so may we forsake every selfish desire
and be ready at all times to answer your call;
through Jesus Christ our Lord.

Alternative Service Book 1980

LOURDES

Since a poor peasant girl, Bernadette Soubirous, received visions of the Blessed Virgin Mary here in 1858, this small town in the foothills of the French Pyrenees has become a popular centre of pilgrimage, particularly for the sick. A spring appeared at the site of the vision, and after miraculous healings were reported of afflicted pilgrims who had been placed in its waters, millions have visited this shrine.

Prayers for pilgrims to Lourdes

O Almighty and everlasting God,
the eternal salvation of those who believe in you,
hear us on behalf of your servants who are sick,
for whom we humbly crave the help of your mercy;
that their health may be restored
    if you see that it is good for them
and that they may render thanks to you
    in your Church,
through Christ our Lord.

Give ear, O Lord, we beseech you,
to our supplications,
and dispose the way of your servants
in the blessedness of your salvation;
that amidst all the various changes
of this our life and pilgrimage,
we may ever be protected by your help.

At the Blessing of the Sick

You said to the paralytic: 'Get up and walk.'
You blessed the sick who were brought to you.
You say to each one of us: 'Come, follow me.'

Response: Lord, that I may walk.

You said to the blind man: 'Go and wash in the
   pool of Siloe.'
You asked the blind man you had healed:
   'Do you believe in the Son of Man?'
You said: 'I am the light of the world.'

Response: Lord, that I may see.

You made the deaf hear and the dumb speak.
You said: 'Listen, anyone who has ears to hear.'
You said: 'Blessed are those who listen to my voice.'

Response: Lord, that I may hear.

When we are in distress,
When we feel helpless,
When we cry out to you,

Response: Lord, hear my cry.

You knew how to give faith to the sick.
   Jesus, we believe in you.
   Jesus, we hope in you.
   Jesus, we love you.

With all Christians,
With those who long for justice,

Response: Lord, we praise you.

'Be still, and know'

Be still, and know I am with you,
be still, I am the Lord.
I will not leave you orphans.
I leave with you my world.
Be one.

You fear the light may be fading,
you fear to lose your way.
Be still, and know I am near you.
I'll lead you to the day
and the sun.

Be glad the day you have sorrow,
be glad, for then you live.
The stars shine only in darkness,
and in your need I give
my peace.

Sister Jude

SISTER JUDE *is a nun at Brentwood Ursuline Convent.*

MEDJUGORJE

On St John the Baptist's day 1981, four young children received a vision of the Blessed Virgin Mary on a hillside near Medjugorje in Yugoslavia. Some other children and their priest also received appearances, which have continued. The messages revealed were requests for peace, conversion, faith, and above all, prayer. Pilgrimages in this spirit have been made to this village during the past decade, and prayers written, of which the following is one:

Jesus,
we know that you are merciful
and that you have offered your heart for us.
It is crowned with thorns
and with our sins.
We know that you implore us constantly
so that we do not go astray.
Jesus,
remember us when we are in sin.
By means of your heart
make all men love one another.
Make hatred disappear from among men.
Show us your love.
We all love you
and want you to protect us
with your shepherd's heart,
and free us from every sin.
Jesus,
enter into every heart.
Knock, knock
at the door of our heart.
Be patient and never desist.

We are still closed
because we have not understood your love.
Knock continuously,
O good Jesus,
Make us open our hearts to you,
at least in the moment
when we remember what your Passion
suffered for us.

ROME

An early Christian community existed in Rome by the middle of the first century AD. St Paul wrote his Epistle to the Corinthians from Rome about AD 58, and he was later imprisoned and put to death here. Tradition asserts that St Peter reached Rome in AD 42, became the first bishop and was also martyred here. As a consequence, Rome has been a place of pilgrimage over the centuries.

Collect for the Conversion of St Paul – 25 January

God, who hast taught the world,
through the preaching of thy blessed apostle Saint
   Paul:
Grant we beseech thee,
that we who have his wonderful conversion in
   remembrance,
may follow and fulfil
thy holy doctrine that he taught;
through Jesus Christ our Lord.

First and Second Books of Common Prayer
of Edward VI, 1549 and 1552

Collect for St Peter the Apostle – 29 June

Almighty God,
who inspired your apostle Saint Peter
to confess Jesus as Christ and Son of the living God:
build up your Church upon this rock,

that in unity and peace
it may proclaim one truth and follow one Lord,
your Son our Saviour Jesus Christ,
who is alive and reigns with you and the Holy Spirit,
One God, now and for ever.

Alternative Service Book 1980

A prayer of Pope Paul VI

May the inner impulse of the Holy Spirit help us to
  direct towards God in the highest,
  the God of all perfection,

our living souls, that his presence may enlighten the
  thought of our minds;
our questing souls, that they may open to the
  revelation of his mysterious wisdom;
our weary souls, that they may be sustained by trust
  in his providence;
our darkened souls, that they may be awakened to
  the brightness of his beauty;
our restless souls, that they may find rest in the
  harmony of his peace;
our sorrowing souls, that they may rise upward
  through self-offering to his goodness;
our guilty souls, that they may be cleansed by the
  tears that his justice has declared blessed;
our unfathomable souls, that they may be overcome
  with joy at his infinite love.

TAIZÉ

In 1942 a small group of men from various Christian traditions established a new ecumenical religious Order, under the leadership of Roger Schulz, a Swiss Protestant; their centre was the Burgundian village of Taizé. The expansion of their work of Christian renewal has been phenomenal, especially among young people who have been drawn in their thousands to share in the simple life-style and new type of worship which has emerged as the spirit of Taizé.

Prayers written by Brother Roger

Lord Christ, gentle and humble of heart
we hear your quiet call:
'You, follow me.'
You give us this vocation
so that together we may live a parable of
    communion
and, having taken the risk of an entire lifetime,
we may be ferments of reconciliation
in that irreplaceable communion
called the Church.
Show us how to respond courageously
without getting trapped
in the quicksand of our hesitations.
Come, so that we may be sustained
by the breath of your Spirit,
the one thing that matters,
without which nothing impels us
to keep on moving forward.

You ask all who know
how to love and suffer with you
to leave themselves behind and follow you.
When, to love with you and not without you,
we must abandon some project contrary to your
    plan,
then come, O Christ,
and fill us with quiet confidence:
make us realise that your love
will never disappear,
and that to follow you means giving our lives.

O Christ,
in every creature you place
first and for ever a word:
God's forgiveness and his confidence in us.
To walk in your footsteps
you offer us the energy always to begin anew.
Following you
through the humble events of every day
means discerning a way —
not a law burdening us with obligations,
but you, O Christ, you are the Way
and on this road God comes to meet us.

Lord Christ, even if we had faith enough to move
    mountains, without living charity, what would
    we be?
You love us.
Without your Spirit who lives in our hearts, what
    would we be?
You love us.
By taking everything upon yourself, you open for
    us a way towards faith, toward trust in God,

who wants neither suffering nor human
distress.

Spirit of the risen Christ, Spirit of compassion,
Spirit of praise, your love for each one will never
disappear.

Spirit of the living God, when our doubts and
hesitations to welcome you seem to submerge
all else, you are there, present for every human
being without exception.

You rekindle the fire smouldering within, beneath
our ashes. You feed this fire with our own
thorns and all that hurts us in ourselves and
others, so that even the stones in our hearts can
become glowing lights in our darkness, dawn in
the depths of our night.

THE NEW WORLD

During the seventeenth century, families opposed to the intolerance of the prevailing religious outlook in England and elsewhere in Europe, turned to America as a place where they could practise their religion as they saw fit. The original 'Pilgrim Fathers' set sail from Plymouth and Delft in the *Mayflower* in 1620. They were followed by others, like Anne Bradstreet and Edward Taylor, who have left prayers and poetry which express their faith in vivid terms. Their work contains not only 'puritan' insights born of travail and persecution, but some of the characteristics of the piety and poetry they had left behind: that of John Donne, George Herbert, Robert Herrick and others. What have been called 'common nutrients' travelled well.

'As weary pilgrim, now at rest'

As weary pilgrim, now at rest,
   Hugs with delight his silent nest,
His wasted limbs now lie full soft
   That miry steps have trodden oft,
Blesses himself to think upon
   His dangers past, and travails done.
The burning sun no more shall heat,
   Nor stormy rains on him shall beat.
The briars and thorns no more shall scratch,
   Nor hungry wolves at him shall catch.
He erring paths no more shall tread,
   Nor wild fruits eat instead of bread.
For waters cold he doth not long,

For thirst no more shall parch his tongue.
No rugged stones his feet shall gall,
  Nor stumps nor rocks cause him to fall.
All cares and fears he bids farewell
  And means in safety now to dwell.
A pilgrim I, on earth perplexed
  With sins, with cares and sorrows vext,
By age and pains brought to decay,
  And my clay house mold'ring away.
Oh, how I long to be at rest
  And soar on high among the blest . . .
And when a few years shall be gone
  This mortal shall be clothed upon.
A corrupt carcase down it lies,
  A glorious body it shall rise.
In weakness and dishonour sown,
  In power 'tis raised by Christ alone.
Then soul and body shall unite
  And of their Maker have the sight.
Such lasting joys shall there behold
  As ear ne'er heard not tongue e'er told.
Lord make me ready for that day,
  Then come, dear Bridegroom, come away.

Anne Bradstreet modernised by J. Wild

The joy of Church fellowship rightly attended

In Heaven soaring up, I dropped an ear
  On earth: and oh sweet melody.
And listening, found it was the Saints who were
  Encoached for Heaven that sang for joy.
  For in Christ's coach they sweetly sing,
  As they to glory ride therein . . .

Some few not in, and some whose time and place
    Block up this Coach's way, do go
As Travellers afoot: and so do trace
    The Road that gives them right thereto;
    While in this Coach these sweetly sing
    As they to Glory ride therein.

Edward Taylor

Columbus

. . . O God, this world, so crammed with eager life,
That comes and goes and wanders back to silence
Like the idle wind, while yet man's shaping mind
Can make his drudge to swell the longing sails
Of highest endeavour . . .
Lets her great destinies be waved aside . . .
If the chosen soul could never be alone
In deep mid-silence, open-doored to God,
No greatness ever had been dreamed or done;
Among dull hearts a prophet never grew;
The nurse of full-grown souls is solitude . . .
          For me, I have no choice;
I might turn back to other destinies,
For one sincere key opes all Fortune's doors;
But whoso answers not God's earliest call
Forfeits or dulls that faculty supreme
Of lying open to his genius
Which makes the wise heart certain of its ends.
Here am I; for what end God knows, not I;
Westward still points the inexorable soul;
Here am I, with no friend but the sad sea,
The beating heart of this great enterprise . . .
          One day more
These muttering shoalbrains leave the helm
    to me . . .

One poor day!
Remember whose and not how short it is!
It is God's day, it is Columbus's.
A lavish day! One day, with life and heart,
Is more than time enough to find a world.

James Russell Lowell

ANNE BRADSTREET *born c. 1612 in Northampton, sailed for America in 1630 on the* Arbella *with her husband Simon Bradstreet and her parents. She began writing religious poetry about this time, though she could not make public this activity 'unseemly for a woman'. They settled in Massachusetts where her husband became governor, and she was well known for her wisdom and devotion to God and her family.*

EDWARD TAYLOR *c. 1645–1729, a Dissenter, was born in Coventry and went to America in his early twenties, to escape the restrictive laws of 1662. He became a Puritan minister in Massachusetts, writing poetry in the style of pre-Restoration religious poets. He married twice and had thirteen children, seven of whom died before him.*

JAMES RUSSELL LOWELL *1819–91, a prolific poet, was born in Cambridge, Massachusetts, and became a professor at Harvard University. He saw Columbus's voyage in terms of a pilgrimage.*

THE HOLY LAND – Beginning the Pilgrimage

Lord Jesus Christ,
you were a pilgrim in this Holy Land.
Now you lead and guide us
on our pilgrimage to the heavenly Jerusalem.

As we follow in your steps,
we ask the grace to keep our eyes on you.
Open our hearts that we may find you,
not only in ancient stones,
but in your people
and in each other.
Let your words be a fire
burning within us.
Write your Gospel upon our hearts.
Give us a spirit of prayer
lest we return full of facts
but not of grace and love.
Lord, teach us to pray
in the very land
where you taught your disciples.

Stephen Doyle OFM

For Jerusalem

O Eternal Lord God, Source of all truth, Lover of
all men, we thank thee for the experience of living
in this city.
Grant that we may be humble, grateful people,
    worshipping people,
    holy people.

Help us to be peace-loving people,
   who know the things that belong to peace,
   who pray and work for peace,
   who try to understand the experiences, the
      hurts, the hopes of people from whom we
      differ.
Let this city be a centre of unity for the Churches.
Let it be a place of friendship and understanding
   for men of different faiths.
Let it be truly the City of Peace, a joy of the
   whole earth and a place of blessing to all nations.
For the sake of him who wept in love over this
   city and died in love outside its walls.
Now the Everliving One, be ever present with thee
   to heal and bless, Jesus Christ our blessed Lord
   and Saviour.

George Appleton

Blessing upon pilgrimage

May the babe of Bethlehem be yours to tend;
May the boy of Nazareth be yours to friend;
May the man of Galilee his healing send;
May the Christ of Calvary his courage lend;
May the Risen Lord his presence send;
And his holy angels defend you, to the end.

Ronald Brownrigg and George Potter

STEPHEN DOYLE OFM *b.1934, is an American member of the Franciscan Order of Friars Minor and regularly leads Holy Land pilgrimages.*

GEORGE APPLETON *b. 1902, see note on p. 4.*

RONALD BROWNRIGG *b. 1919, is an Honorary Canon of Southwark Cathedral and has led many pilgrimages to the Holy Land. He adapted this prayer from the words of Father George Potter of Peckham.*

BETHLEHEM

'. . . and Joseph went up . . . to the city of David, which is called Bethlehem, because he was of the house and lineage of David, to be enrolled with Mary, his betrothed, who was with child. And while they were there, the time came for her to be delivered. And she gave birth to her first-born son and wrapped him in swaddling cloths, and laid him in a manger, because there was no place for them in the inn.' *Luke* 2.4–7

Bethlehem, of noblest cities
  None can once with thee compare;
Thou alone the Lord from heaven
  Didst for us incarnate bear.

Fairer than the sun at morning
  Was the star that told his birth;
To the lands their God announcing,
  Hid beneath a form of earth.

By its lambent beauty guided
  See the eastern kings appear;
See them bend, their gifts to offer,
  Gifts of incense, gold and myrrh.

Solemn things of mystic meaning:
  Incense doth the God disclose,
Gold a royal child proclaimeth,
  Myrrh a future tomb foreshows.

Holy Jesu, in thy brightness
To the Gentile world displayed,
With the Father and the Spirit
Endless praise to thee be paid.

Prudentius, translated by Edward Caswall

Child of Bethlehem,
What contrasts you embrace!
No one has ever been so humble;
no one has ever wielded such power.
We stand in awe of your holiness,
and yet we are bathed in your love.

And where shall we look for you?
You are in high heaven,
in the glory of the Godhead.
Yet those who searched for you on earth
found you in a tiny baby at Mary's breast.
We come in hushed reverence to find you as God,
and you welcome us as man.
We come unthinkingly to find you as man,
and are blinded by the light of your Godhead . . .
We need you, above anything in the world.

Ephraem of Syria

It is indeed right and proper,
it is only fitting and what our duty requires of us,
that always and everywhere,
we should give you thanks,
holy Lord, almighty Father, eternal God:

For a marvellous change was wrought in our nature
    at its restoration.
This truth flashed on the world when
    from the old stock the new Man was born,
    from mortality to immortality,
    from human nature the remedy was drawn
    for human nature's healing;
From a race of sinners sprang a child
    who was innocent of sin.
When your Word took to himself
    this frail nature of ours,
    it was honoured with the gift of eternity
    and we ourselves, sharing its wonderful destiny,
    were made eternal also.

Through him the angels offer their praise of your
        majesty,
    the lordships their veneration,
    the powers their awe-struck reverence;
Through him the heavens, the powers in the
        heavens,
    and the blessed seraphim,
    exulting together, adore you.
Grant, we pray you, that our voices too,
    may gain a hearing with theirs,
    as we humbly confess you and say,
'Holy, Holy, Holy, Lord God of Hosts,
Heaven and earth are full of your glory.
Glory be to you, O Lord most high.'

Leonine Sacramentary

Your nativity, O Christ our God,
has revealed to the world
the light of wisdom;
for in it those who worshipped the stars
were taught by a star to adore you,
the Sun of Righteousness,
and to know you,
the Dayspring from on high.
Glory be to you, O Lord.

The Virgin today gives birth to him
who is above all creation;
and the earth offers the cave to him
whom none can approach unto.
Angels and shepherds sing glory,
and wise men journey with a star,
since for our sake has come
as a new-born Child, he who from all eternity is
    God.

Eastern Orthodox Prayer

O God, our gracious heavenly Father,
Creator and Sustainer,
and yet our Father,
we thank you on this wonderful day
for that little Child
who would make us all your sons.
As we remember his lowly, humble birth,
take away our pride.
As we remember his pure life,
take away our sins.

As we remember how he came,
not to be ministered unto, but to minister,
help us to serve more unselfishly,
give more generously,
and love more devotedly. For his sake.

Leslie Weatherhead

PRUDENTIUS *348–c. 410 was a Spanish poet and hymn-writer. The hymn 'Bethlehem, of noblest cities' was translated from the Latin by Edward Caswall 1814–78.*

EPHRAEM OF SYRIA *c. 306–373 was a Syrian biblical exegete based on Edessa, who wrote exclusively in Syriac.*

THE LEONINE SACRAMENTARY, *of the early seventh century, is the earliest surviving book of Mass prayers according to the Roman rite.*

LESLIE WEATHERHEAD *1893–1976, see note on p. 40.*

NAZARETH

'. . . Nazareth, where he had been brought up . . .'
Luke 4.16

'Many who heard him were astonished, saying . . . "Is
not this the carpenter, the son of Mary?"' *Mark 6.2–3*

Almighty God,
who did ordain that your Son Jesus Christ
should labour with his hands to suppy his own
     needs,
and the needs of others:
Teach us, we pray you, that no labour is mean,
and all labour is divine,
to which you call us;
to the glory of your holy Name.

Eric Milner-White

Jesus, Master Carpenter of Nazareth,
who worked on the cross
through wood and nails
our whole salvation:
Wield your tools well
in this your workshop;
that we who come to you rough hewn
may by your hand be fashioned
to a truer beauty and a greater usefulness,
for the honour of your name.

ERIC MILNER-WHITE *1884–1963, see note on p. 15.*
*'Jesus, Master Carpenter of Nazareth' was written during the First
World War and is often attributed to Hal Pink of Toc H.*

THE RIVER JORDAN

'In those days Jesus came from Nazareth of Galilee and was baptised by John in the Jordan . . .' *Mark 1.9*

Almighty God,
who at the baptism of thy blessed Son Jesus Christ
in the river Jordan
didst manifest his glorious Godhead;
Grant, we beseech thee,
that the brightness of his presence
may shine in our hearts,
and his glory be set forth in our lives,
through the same Jesus Christ our Lord.

Scottish Prayer Book

When you were baptised in Jordan,
O Lord,
then was made manifest
the worship of the Trinity;
for the Voice of the Father
bore witness to you,
naming you his beloved Son;
and the Spirit
in form of a dove
made certainty of his word.
O Christ our God,
who was manifested
and has enlightened the world,
glory be to you.

You are manifested today
to the whole world,
and your light, O Lord,
has been shown upon us,
who hymn you of full knowledge.
You are come,
You are manifest,
You who are the Light inaccessible.

Eastern Orthodox Prayers

Antiphon: A soldier baptises the king;
a servant baptises his master;
John baptises his creator.
The water of Jordan is amazed;
the dove bears witness;
the voice of the Father is heard:
'This is my beloved son,
in whom I am well-pleased. Hear him.'

Collect: God, creator and redeemer of all souls,
who for the salvation of the human race
wished to be baptised
in the water of Jordan,
graciously grant
that we should venerate the mystery,
and pursue the grace
of your sacred baptism.

*Processionals of the fifteenth century compiled
by the Franciscans of Mount Sion*

THE LAKE OF GALILEE

'He said to them, "Follow me, and I will make you fishers of men." Immediately they left their nets and followed him.' *Matthew 4.19–20*

The calling of the disciples

Dear Lord and Father of mankind,
    Forgive our foolish ways!
Re-clothe us in our rightful mind,
In purer lives thy service find,
    In deeper reverence praise.

In simple trust like theirs who heard,
    Beside the Syrian sea,
The gracious calling of the Lord,
Let us, like them, without a word
    Rise up and follow thee.

O Sabbath rest by Galilee!
    O calm of hills above,
Where Jesus knelt to share with thee
The silence of eternity,
    Interpreted by love!

Drop thy still dews of quietness,
    Till all our strivings cease;
Take from our souls the strain and stress,
And let our ordered lives confess
    The beauty of thy peace.

Breathe through the heats of our desire
    Thy coolness and thy balm;

Let sense be dumb, let flesh retire;
Speak through the earthquake, wind, and fire,
　　O still small voice of calm!

J. G. Whittier

The feeding of the multitude at Tabgha

O you who clothe the lilies
and feed the birds of the air,
who lead the lambs to pasture
and the hart to the water's side.

Who has multiplied loaves and fishes
and converted water into wine,
come to our table,
as giver and guest to dine.

Stephen Doyle OFM

JOHN GREENLEAF WHITTIER *1802–92, an American Quaker, farmer, journalist and poet, was from 1836 Secretary of the American Anti-Slavery League.*

STEPHEN DOYLE *b. 1934, see note on p. 107.*

BETHANY

'Six days before the Passover, Jesus came to Bethany,
where Lazarus was, whom Jesus had raised from the
dead . . . The next day a great crowd who had come to
the feast heard that Jesus was coming to Jerusalem.
So they took branches of palm trees and went out
to meet him, crying, "Hosanna! Blessed is he who
comes in the name of the Lord!"' *John 12.1, 12–13*

O Christ our God,
before your Passion
you confirmed the truth
of the general resurrection
by raising Lazarus from the dead.
Therefore we also,
like the children bearing the symbols of triumph,
cry out to you,
the conqueror of death:
'Hosanna in the highest.
Blessed is he who comes in the name of the Lord.'

Seated upon the throne in heaven
and upon the colt on earth,
O Christ our God,
you accepted the praise of the angels
and the songs of the children
who cried out to you.
Blessed are you who came
to recall Adam from the dead.

Eastern Orthodox Prayers

'When the hour came, he sat at table, and the apostles with him. And he said to them, "I have earnestly desired to eat this passover with you before I suffer; for I tell you I shall not eat it until it is fulfilled in the kingdom of God."' *Luke 22.14–16*

Prayer for Holy Thursday

At thy mystical supper,
Son of God,
today receive me as a partaker;
for I will not speak of the mystery
to thine enemies;
I will not give thee a kiss like Judas;
but like the thief
I will acknowledge thee;
Remember me, Lord,
when thou comest in thy Kingdom.

Prayer Book of the Eastern Orthodox Church

Antiphon: O holy feast in which Christ is
     received;
the mind recalls his passion;
is filled with grace,
and he gives to us a pledge of future
     glory.
Bread from heaven has been bestowed;
containing in itself all sweetness.

Collect: God, who in this most holy chamber,
left to us the holy memory
    of your wonderful passion;
bestow on us, we pray, the power to
    revere
the sacred mysteries of your body and
    blood,
that we should feel in us continually
the fruit of our redemption.

*Processionals of the fifteenth century compiled by
the Franciscans of Mount Sion*

JERUSALEM – Gethsemane

'. . . he fell on his face and prayed, "My Father, if it be possible, let this cup pass from me; nevertheless, not as I will but as thou wilt."' *Matthew 26.39*

O Saviour Christ,
who, in great heaviness of soul
before thy passion,
didst fall down in prayer to thy heavenly Father;
give us grace that we also,
in all troubles of this world,
may run evermore
by most humble and instant prayer
unto the aid and comfort of our heavenly Father;
for thy name's sake.

The Primer of 1559

'*His words to Christ, going to the Cross*'

When thou wast taken, Lord, I oft have read,
All thy disciples thee forsook and fled.
Let their example not a pattern be
For me to fly, but now to follow thee.

Robert Herrick

ROBERT HERRICK *1591–1674, see note on p. 52.*

JERUSALEM – The Church of the Holy Sepulchre

Within its walls are contained the accepted site of Golgotha, the scene of the crucifixion; and the tomb of Jesus, from which he rose on the third day. The church is known by the Eastern Orthodox Church as the Church of the Resurrection.

'In the place where he was crucified there was a garden, and in the garden a new tomb . . . So they laid Jesus there.' *John 19.41–2*

. . . We think that Paradise and Calvary,
   Christ's Cross, and Adam's tree, stood in one
     place;
Look Lord, and find both Adams met in me;
   As the first Adam's sweat surrounds my face,
   May the last Adam's blood my soul embrace.

So, in his purple wrapped receive me Lord,
   By these his thorns give me his other crown;
And as to others' souls I preached thy word,
   Be this my text, my sermon to mine own,
   Therefore that he may raise the Lord throws
     down.

John Donne

At Calvary

O soul, look well
    and count the cost of love,
    lest you your pilgrimage begin
    and lacking love may perish on the way,
    for love alone can reach to love
    and reaching bear the judgment of love's fire.

Love by love alone is perfect made,
    for love is living out in love the call of love,
    for love is an exchange of love
    resolved in will and signified by deed;
    for deed without will is loveless act,
    and will without deed falls short,
    to die stillborn through sinful negligence
    and lack of love's exchange.
            Love, give me love.

Gilbert Shaw

Antiphon: After they crucified Jesus,
            the soldiers received his clothing,
            allotting a portion to each man.
            They divided my clothes for
                themselves;
            and cast lots for my garments.

Collect: Gracious Jesus Christ,
            who for our redemption undertook
            not only to be hanged naked
            from the cross and die,
            by the wicked hands of sinners,
            but even allowed that your most sacred
                garments
            should be allotted and bestowed;

grant that despatched of our vices
and clad in virtue,
we should be worthy to be presented to
    you,
living and true God,
in the glory of heaven.

*Processionals of the 15th century compiled by
the Franciscans of Mount Sion*

Traditional prayer at Golgotha

We adore thee, O Christ,
and we praise thee,
because by thy Cross and Passion
thou hast redeemed the world.

Collect for Good Friday

Almighty God,
we beseech thee graciously to behold
this thy family,
for which our Lord Jesus Christ
was contented to be betrayed,
and given up into the hands of wicked men,
and to suffer death upon the cross,
who now liveth and reigneth with thee
and the Holy Ghost,
ever one God, world without end.

Book of Common Prayer 1662

Prayer for 'Holy and Great Friday'

Thou hast redeemed us from the curse of the law
    by thy precious blood.

Having been nailed to the cross
  and pierced with the spear,
thou hast shed immortality on men.
O, our Saviour, glory to thee.

Prayer for 'Holy and Great Saturday'

When thou didst condescend unto death,
  O Life immortal,
then didst thou slay Hades
  with the lightning of thy divinity;
and when thou didst raise the dead
  from the lower-most parts,
all the heavenly powers cried,
'O Christ, Giver of Life, our God,
  Glory to thee.'

Prayer Book of the Eastern Orthodox Church

O God,
as we bow at the foot of the cross,
may the love that was manifested there
stream into our hearts,
challenging and subduing them
and winning from us that response
which is your will for us.
Through Jesus Christ our Lord.

Leslie Weatherhead

Hymn of the Cross

We bow before thy cross,
O Master,
and we glorify
thy holy resurrection.

Eastern Orthodox Church

Antiphon:	Christ rose early on the Sabbath morning,
	and appeared first to Mary Magdalen
	from whom he cast out seven demons.
	'Mary, touch me not.
	I have not yet risen to my Father.'

Collect:	Most gracious Jesus Christ, Alpha and Omega,
	who early on the Sabbath morning
	brought yourself, gentle with friendly discourse,
	and your longed-for face,
	to Mary Magdalen as she wept sweet tears for you,
	grant to us, unworthy servants,
	that by the merits of your resurrection,
	we should be worthy to see
	your most sweet countenance,
	full of grace, in heavenly glory.

*Processionals of the 15th century compiled by
the Franciscans of Mount Sion*

On Easter

Most glorious Lord of life, that on this day
   didst make thy triumph over death and sin:
   and having harrowed hell, didst bring away
   captivity thence captive us to win:
This joyous day, dear Lord, with joy begin,
   and grant that we for whom thou diddest die,
   being with thy dear blood clean washed from sin,
   may live for ever in felicity.
And that thy love we weighing worthily,
   may likewise love thee for the same again:

and for thy sake that all like dear didst buy,
    with love may one another entertain.
So let us love, dear love, like as we ought,
    love is the lesson which the Lord us taught.

Edmund Spenser

O Christ, risen and glorified,
reigning at God's right hand,
but still our Friend and Saviour,
abide with us,
so that by the loving influence
of your Spirit on our own,
we may become more like you;
until all our selfishness and unkindness
are purged away, and we become
the kind of people whom you can use
in your redeeming and glorious work.
Take possession of us now
and use us henceforth for your glory.
For your name's sake.

Leslie Weatherhead

JOHN DONNE *1573–1631, see note on p. 34. This is taken from his poem, 'Hymn to God, my God, in my Sickness'. In ancient tradition the place of Adam's death is identified with Calvary.*

GILBERT SHAW *1886–1967 was a notable writer, spiritual counsellor and conductor of retreats.*

EDMUND SPENSER *℔1552–99, one of the great poets of the Elizabethan age. This sonnet is from his* Amoretti, lxviii.

LESLIE WEATHERHEAD *1893–1976, see note on p. 40.*

JERUSALEM – The Mount of the Ascension

'. . . and lifting up his hands he blessed them. While he blessed them, he parted from them, and was carried up into heaven.' *Luke 24.51*

O God, who by thy marvellous majesty
didst after thy resurrection from the dead
ascend into heaven in the presence of thine apostles:
Grant us the aid of thy loving kindness,
that according to thy promise
thou mayest ever dwell with us on earth
and we with thee in heaven;
where with the Father and the Holy Spirit
thou reignest God for ever and ever.

Gelasian Sacramentary

Ascended Lord Jesus, we adore you.
Once you lived a human life subject to the
    limitations of time:
  now you are the same yesterday, today and for
    ever.
Once you were limited to one particular place:
  now you are present wherever men turn to you.
Once only those who met you face to face knew you:
  now your divine love extends through all the
    world.

Jesus, ascended Lord of time and space,
   love as wide as life,
   we adore you.

Caryl Micklem
(Editor)

THE GELASIAN SACRAMENTARY *is now considered wrongly attributed to Pope Gelasius (d. 496), but of early date; it was widely circulated in Gaul in the eighth century.*

CARYL MICKLEM *b. 1925, is a retired URC Minister, hymn writer and religious broadcaster.*

JERUSALEM – The Upper Room – Pentecost

'When the day of Pentecost had come, they were all together in one place . . . and they were all filled with the Holy Spirit.' *Acts 2.1,4*

Antiphon: And when the days of Pentecost were
              drawing to a close,
          they were all together in one place.
          And suddenly there came a sound from
              heaven,
          as of a violent wind coming,
          and it filled the whole house
          where they were sitting.
          They were all filled with the Holy
              Spirit;
          and began to speak.

Collect: God, who in this most sacred place
          did teach the hearts of thy faithful
              people
          by the light of thy Holy Spirit,
          grant us by the same Spirit,
          to have a right judgment in all things,
          and ever to rejoice in his consolation.

Processionals of the 15th century compiled by
the Franciscans of Mount Sion

Come, Holy Ghost, our souls inspire,
And lighten with celestial fire.
Thou the anointing Spirit art,
Who dost thy sevenfold gifts impart.

Thy blessèd unction from above
Is comfort, life, and fire of love;
Enable with perpetual light
The dulness of our blinded sight.

Anoint and cheer our soilèd face
With the abundance of thy grace:
Keep far our foes, give peace at home:
Where thou art guide, no ill can come.

Teach us to know the Father, Son,
And thee, of both, to be but One;
That, through the ages all along,
This may be our endless song:

> 'Praise to thy eternal merit,
> Father, Son, and Holy Spirit.'

John Cosin

JOHN COSIN *1594–1672 was Bishop of Durham from 1660. This
translation of the ancient Latin hymn,* Veni Creator, *was included
in the Ordinal in the 1662 Book of Common Prayer.*

THE HOLY LAND – The End of the Pilgrimage

Prayer at the end of a pilgrimage

Father, we have walked in the land where Jesus
  walked.
We have touched the soil and rocks where the seed
  falls.
We have seen the lilies of the field and heard the
  birds of the air.
We have been warmed by the sun that warmed him
  and
cooled by the breezes that touched his face.
We have been to the sea where he walked,
and to the river where he was baptised.
We have felt the presence of the Holy Spirit
where he first sent it,
and anguished at the spot where he gave himself for
  us.
We have rejoiced at the emptiness of the tomb
and the fulness of his love in our hearts.
Be with us, as we continue our earthly pilgrimage
to the new Jerusalem
where every tear will be wiped away,
and we will be with you, your Son and the Holy
  Spirit forever.

Stephen Doyle OFM

STEPHEN DOYLE *b. 1934, see note on p. 107.*

A Prayer for Peace in the Holy Land

O Lord soften the stone hearts
of those who preach and practise
intolerance and bigotry;
as the sun's setting glow
softens the stone walls
of your Holy City, Jerusalem.

     Lord, the rocky hills, the valleys
     the deserts and the sea shores
     are filled with the echoes of
     centuries of pain.

Lord, bring peace to house and village.
Comfort the mothers who fret
and those who mourn.
Lord, keep strong the twisted old root
of the olive tree,
and protect the young vine.

     Lord of water and stone,
     of bread and wine,
     Lord of resurrection,
     feed hope, and bring peace
     to this wracked but beautiful holy land.

Gerald Butt

GERALD BUTT *wrote this prayer when a BBC correspondent in Israel.*

Index of Sources and Places

ACKNOWLEDGEMENTS

The compiler and publishers are pleased to acknowledge the following for permission to quote from their copyright material:

David Adam, for 'For St Cuthbert', 'For St Aidan', 'For St Bede' and 'For the Holy Island of Lindisfarne'.

Ronald Brownrigg, for 'Blessing upon pilgrimage' which was adapted from a prayer by Father George Potter of Peckham.

Gerald Butt, for 'A Prayer for Peace in the Holy Land'.

Cassell/Mowbray for 'Lord Christ, gentle and humble of heart', from *Parable of Community* by Brother Roger (1980), and for 'Lord Christ, even if we had faith enough', from *The Taizé Experience* (1990).

The Central Board of Finance of the Church of England, for the collects of St Peter and St James, from *The Alternative Service Book 1980*.

The Church Missionary Society, for 'O God our Father', 'O Jesus, be the canoe that holds me' and 'O God, we pray to you', from *Morning, Noon and Night* by John Carden (1976).

Darton, Longman & Todd, for the prayer from Medjugorje, from *The Fountain Within* by Robert Llewelyn (1989).

Eyre & Spottiswoode/Cambridge University Press, for a collect for Good Friday from *The Book of Common Prayer* (1662), the rights of which are vested in the Crown in perpetuity.

Faber & Faber, for lines from *Little Gidding*, I, from *Collected Poems 1909–1962* by T. S. Eliot (1963).

The Liturgical Press for 'Lord Jesus Christ, you were a pilgrim', 'O you who clothe the lilies' and 'Father, we have walked in the land where Jesus walked', from *The Pilgrim's New Guide to the Holy Land* by Stephen Doyle (1985).

A Hamman (editor) for the prayer of Clement of Alexandria and the excerpt from the Leonine Sacramentary, from *Early Christian Prayers* (Longman, 1961).

Sister Jude, Brentwood Ursuline Convent, for 'Be still, and know I am with you'.

The Little Gidding Community, for an extract from their 'Undertakings'.

Caryl Micklem (editor), for 'Ascended, Lord Jesus, we adore you', from *Contemporary Prayers for Public Worship* (SCM Press, 1967).

Oxford University Press, for the translation of St Thomas Aquinas' 'O creator past all telling', from *The Oxford Book of Prayer*, edited by George Appleton (1985); and for 'Teach us, your servants and pilgrims' from *Daily Prayer*, edited by Eric Milner-White and G. W. Briggs (1941); and for 'Alone with none by thee, my God', from *English Praise*.

Paulinus Press, for two prayers for pilgrims to St David's from *A Pilgrim's Manual*, edited by Brian Brendan O'Malley (1985).

Penguin Books, for the excerpt from *Proslogion*, from *Prayers and Meditations of St Anselm*, translated by Sister Benedicta Ward (1973).

Bryn A. Rees, for 'Have faith in God'.

St Peter's Pilgrims, for 'At the blessing of the Sick', from *The Lourdes Prayer Book*.

The Sisters of the Love of God, Fairacres, Oxford, for 'O soul, look well' from *A Pilgrim's Book of Prayers* by Gilbert Shaw (1945).

SPCK, for extracts from *Francis and Clare: The Complete Works* by R. J. Armstrong and I. C. Brady (1982); for 'For Jerusalem', from *Jerusalem Prayers* by George Appleton (1974); for 'Lord, you are God', from *Julian of Norwich: Showings*, edited by E. Colledge and J. Walsh (1978); and for 'Control me, O my God' from *My God, My Glory* by Eric Milner-White (1954).

Stainer & Bell, for 'Now let us from this table rise', from *Pilgrim Praise* by Frederick Kaan (1968).

John V. Taylor, for 'Lord Jesus Christ, alive and at large in the world', from *A Matter of Life and Death* (SCM Press, 1986).

Triangle Books (SPCK), for 'Listen, O Lord', from *Another Day* by John Carden (1986); for the prayer by Walter Hilton, from *Praying With the English Mystics*, compiled by Jenny Robertson (1990); and for 'May God be with you in every pass' and 'Before me be thou a smooth way', from *Praying With Highland Christians* by G. R. D. McLean (1961, 1988).

The estate of Leslie Weatherhead for five prayers from *A Private House of Prayer* (Arthur James, 1985).

R. R. Williams (translator), for 'Though my path repels my nature', from *Hymns of Ann Griffiths* (The Brython Press).

David Winter, for extracts from *The Shepherd* of Hermas and from Ephraem of Syria, from *After the Gospels* (Mowbrays, 1977).